Carlean Johnson

CJ
BOOKS
Washington

Six Ingredients Or Less

Cover design and art direction: Gregory E. Hickman
Typography and production design: Linda Hazen

ISBN 0-942878-00-0

C. J. Books
P.O. Box 922
Gig Harbor, WA 98335
206-851-3778

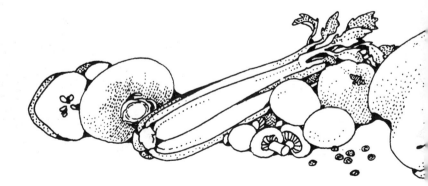

This book is dedicated to my sons Brian and Mike who never knew what they were going to have for dinner and whose comments ran from "Yuk" to "Put it in the cookbook, Mom" and to my daughter Linda who shares my love for cooking.

ACKNOWLEDGEMENTS

I would like to thank the many friends and relatives who shared their recipes and ideas. Also the cooks who have so enthusiastically enjoyed the first edition of this cookbook and have shared their thoughts, experiences and recipes with me.

A special thanks to Gregory Hickman, who came to my rescue at almost the last minute, and came through with the beautiful cover design and art direction. Greg, you were a lifesaver.

And most of all I want to thank my daughter Linda Hazen, for all her hard work, long hours and dedication to the revision of this book. Fortunately she learned extremely fast and was able to do the work on the computer in less time than many more experienced professionals could have. I couldn't have done it without you.

TABLE OF CONTENTS

Basic Recipe for Using this Book

1) Always read through the recipe first. Then assemble and measure the ingredients before you start. These simple steps will save you a lot of time.

2) If necessary, remove butter and cream cheese from refrigerator to allow time to soften. Also remove eggs.

3) Most of the recipes can be cut in half or doubled.

4) The number of servings is not necessarily the same as the number of people to be served; this can vary according to individual appetites.

5) Eggs are easier to separate when cold, but whites should be beaten when at room temperature.

6) Clarified butter (see Index) is best for browning meats, fish, poultry, etc. since it doesn't burn as easily.

7) Since we don't always have time to make pie crust from scratch, there are some very acceptable prepared ones on the market. But for a special occasion, you will get a lot of satisfaction from making your own.

8) Keep a well-stocked pantry for last minute entertaining. It doesn't have to be fancy, just good.

INTRODUCTION

This is the cookbook for the cook who never has enough time. Time or lack of it, is a problem for many of us. Yet there is a concern about feeding our family well and selecting foods that are quick and nutritious as well as pleasing to everyone. This is a collection of recipes designed for the busy person who wants to serve tasty dishes with a minimum of time and effort. Included are basic recipes for everyday cooking as well as those for special occasions and holiday entertaining. Not only will you save time, but hopefully money as well.

      With our ever changing lifestyles, we do not have time to spend long hours in the kitchen planning meals from lengthy and complicated recipes. I saw a real need for a different type of cookbook; one that would get you in and out of the kitchen fast and yet could be a gourmet's delight or just a simple Sunday dinner. People I interviewed wanted to use basic types of foods they normally have on hand. They didn't have a lot of time to spend in the kitchen and many wanted to be able to share cooking responsibilities. Thus was born SIX INGREDIENTS OR LESS, a one of a kind cookbook that you will enjoy even if you are not in a hurry.

      After six years, it was time to revise and redesign SIX INGREDIENTS OR LESS. Recipes have been updated. Favorite time-tested recipes have remained and over 200 new recipes have been included. Every kitchen needs a book that belongs out on the counter where it can become worn with frequent use. This is that type of cookbook. It was written to be used daily for most of your cooking needs. Add your own personal touches and who would guess you hadn't spent all day in the kitchen. Cooking needn't be a chore and can be fun. Let others help in the preparation and time in the kitchen can be kept to a minimum.

These recipes are enjoyed in my kitchen and they can be enjoyed in yours.

                        Happy Cooking!

                        Carlean Johnson
                        Gig Harbor, Washington

Appetizers & Beverages

FROSTY FRUIT CUPS FREEZE

2 cups ginger ale
1 (6-ounce) can frozen orange juice concentrate
1 (12-ounce) can frozen pineapple chunks
1 cup green seedless grapes
$^1/_2$ cup Maraschino cherry halves
2 cups cantaloupe balls

Combine ginger ale and orange juice concentrate; stir until dissolved. Pour into small container. Freeze just to a mush, about $1^1/_2$ to 2 hours. Partially thaw pineapple (some ice crystals should remain). Combine pineapple with remaining fruit. Stir ginger ale mixture; spoon into 8 sherbet dishes; top with fruit. Makes 8 servings.
TIP: Timing is important in this recipe, but it is worth the effort.

PUMPKIN SEED SNACKS OVEN

2 cups pumpkin seeds
1 tablespoon oil
1 tablespoon melted butter
Salt

Wipe fibers from pumpkin seeds, but do not wash. Combine oil and melted butter and pour over seeds; toss to coat. Spread out on large baking sheet. Sprinkle with salt. Bake at 350° for 30 minutes or until golden brown and crisp. Cool. Store in covered container. Makes 2 cups.

FRIED CAMEMBERT TOP OF STOVE

1 ($4^1/_2$-ounce) round Camembert cheese, chilled
1 egg, lightly beaten
$^1/_2$ cup fine fresh bread crumbs
Oil, about 2 tablespoons

Do not remove rind from cheese. Dip in egg and then in bread crumbs. If necessary pat on extra bread crumbs to coat. Heat oil in small skillet. Cook on both sides until a nice golden brown. Serve hot. Makes 4 servings.
TIP: Delicious served with plain crackers and salsa or raspberry preserves.

TERIYAKI STRIPS

MARINATE
BROIL OR
GRILL

    2 pounds top round beef, partially frozen
    $^1/_2$ cup peanut oil (or other oil)
    $^1/_2$ cup soy sauce
    $^1/_2$ cup dry sherry
    1 tablespoon freshly grated ginger
    1 small garlic clove, minced

Cut beef crosswise into thin strips. Combine remaining ingredients in shallow dish. Add beef strips and marinate 2 to 3 hours. Place beef strips accordion style on bamboo sticks or metal skewers. Grill or broil. TIP: Soak bamboo skewers in water to prevent them from burning.

CHILDREN'S BIRD SEED

A great school snack when it's your child's turn to supply the treat. Watch carefully, the M&M's always go first!

    2 cups Sugar Pops cereal
    $^1/_2$ cup raisins
    $^1/_2$ cup peanuts
    $^1/_2$ cup M&M's candies

Mix ingredients in large bowl and serve as a snack. Makes $3^1/_2$ cups.

PINEAPPLE CHEESE BALLS

CHILL

A most requested recipe during the holidays.

    2 (8-ounce) packages cream cheese, softened
    1 (8-ounce) can crushed pineapple, drained
    2 cups finely chopped pecans or walnuts
    $^1/_4$ cup finely chopped green pepper
    2 tablespoons finely chopped onion
    1 tablespoon seasoned salt

In mixer bowl, beat cream cheese until smooth. Add crushed pineapple, 1 cup of the nuts, green pepper, onion and salt; mix well. (If using food processor, do not overmix.) Cover and chill until firm enough to shape. Divide mixture in half; shape into balls and roll in remaining 1 cup of nuts. Cover and chill several hours or overnight. Serve with assorted crackers. Makes 2 cheese balls.
TIP: Left over cheese balls can be reshaped and rolled in additional nuts. For a variation from the traditional cheese ball, place mixture in small serving bowl or crock and serve at room temperature. (Do not use the second cup of nuts.)

SESAME CHEESE BALL   CHILL

1 (8-ounce) package cream cheese, softened
$^1/_2$ cup grated Cheddar cheese
1 tablespoon finely chopped green pepper
1 teaspoon Worcestershire sauce
$^1/_3$ cup finely chopped walnuts
$^1/_3$ cup lightly toasted sesame seeds

Combine first 5 ingredients in mixer bowl or food processor; mix until blended. Chill until firm enough to shape. Shape into ball; roll in sesame seeds. Cover and chill until ready to serve. Makes 1 cheese ball.

APRICOT ALMOND BRIE   TOP OF STOVE

Elegant but very quick and easy. Serve with a plain type cracker.

1 (8 to 10-ounce) wedge Brie cheese
$^1/_2$ cup apricot preserves
1 tablespoon Grand Marnier liqueur
1 tablespoon toasted sliced almonds

Remove top rind from cheese. Place cheese on serving plate. In small saucepan, combine preserves and liqueur. Heat until mixture is hot, but do not boil. Pour some of the sauce over cheese (save remainder for adding later, if desired). Sprinkle almonds over top. Makes 4 to 6 servings.

WATER CHESTNUT APPETIZERS   MARINATE
                                               OVEN

1 (8-ounce) can water chestnuts
$^1/_4$ cup soy sauce
$^1/_4$ cup sugar
1 pound lean bacon

Cut water chestnuts in 2 or 3 pieces depending on size of chestnut. Combine soy sauce and sugar in small dish; add chestnuts and marinate 30 minutes, stirring occasionally. Cut bacon slices in half crosswise and lengthwise. Remove chestnuts from marinade. Wrap each chestnut with 2 strips of bacon; secure with wooden toothpick. Arrange on rack in shallow baking pan. Bake at 400° for 20 to 30 minutes or until bacon is crisp. Drain on paper towels. Makes 3 to 4 dozen.
TIP: Can be prepared ahead, then baked, or baked and reheated in oven or microwave.

CREAM CHEESE WITH TOPPING

**Place an 8-ounce block of cream cheese on serving dish and
top with one of the following:**
Chutney
Green Pepper Jelly
Shrimp or crab in cocktail sauce

Serve with assorted crackers.

QUICK CRAB COCKTAIL

Crabmeat, small chunks
Bottled cocktail sauce
Shredded lettuce

Combine crabmeat and cocktail sauce. Place shredded lettuce in small
cocktail cups; top with crab.
TIP: To substitute, use tiny shrimp for the crab.

SWEET AND SOUR WRAP-UPS   OVEN

1 pound lean bacon
2 (8-ounce) cans water chestnuts, drained
1¹/₂ cups catsup
²/₃ cup sugar
¹/₄ cup fresh lemon juice

Cut bacon crosswise into thirds. Cut small water chestnuts in half and
larger ones in thirds. Wrap 1 piece of bacon around each water chestnut. Secure bacon with wooden toothpicks. Place in 9x13-inch baking
dish. Bake at 350° for 30 minutes or until bacon is crisp (do not over
cook). Drain off fat. Combine remaining ingredients; pour over bacon.
Reduce heat to 325° and bake 20 to 30 minutes, basting once or twice.
Serve hot. Makes about 4 dozen.
TIP: These go fast. For a large group make a double recipe. You can
prepare the bacon and water chestnuts ahead; cover and refrigerate.
Mix sauce; cover and set aside.

DOROTHY'S COCONUT CHIPS   OVEN

A wonderful company snack served in your prettiest serving bowls.

> **1 coconut**
> **1¹/₂ teaspoons melted butter**
> **Salt**

Pierce eyes of coconut; drain milk. Bake at 350° for 30 minutes. Break coconut open with hammer. Trim off brown skin. Shave coconut into thin strips with vegetable peeler. Spread chips on large baking sheet. Bake at 250° for 1 to 1¹/₂ hours or until just lightly toasted. Chips should be very light in color with just a touch of brown around the edges. Drizzle melted butter over chips, sprinkle lightly with salt, and toss to coat. Makes 1¹/₂ to 2 cups.

SHRIMP WITH SAUCE   CHILL

> **Fresh cooked shrimp, chilled**
> **¹/₂ cup catsup**
> **¹/₂ cup chili sauce**
> **2 tablespoons horseradish**
> **2 teaspoons lemon juice**
> **Dash Tabasco sauce**

Combine last 5 ingredients until blended. Cover and chill until ready to serve. Pour sauce into small serving dish; surround with shrimp and serve with cocktail picks. Makes 1¹/₄ cups sauce.

BAKED CHICKEN NUGGETS   OVEN

Adapts well for a crowd. Just double or triple the recipe.

> **2 whole chicken breasts, skinned and boned**
> **1¹/₂ cups fine dry bread crumbs**
> **¹/₃ cup grated Parmesan cheese**
> **¹/₂ teaspoon salt**
> **¹/₂ teaspoon dried basil or oregano (optional)**
> **¹/₂ cup butter or margarine, melted**

Cut chicken breasts into about 1¹/₂-inch squares. Combine dry ingredients in small bowl. Dip chicken pieces in melted butter, then in crumb mixture. Pat crumbs on to coat. Place on greased baking sheet and bake at 400° for 15 to 20 minutes or until lightly browned. Makes about 36.

HERRING APPETIZERS

Herring tidbits
Sour cream
Crackers

Combine herring and sour cream and serve with crackers.

COCKTAIL PECANS   OVEN

2 cups pecans
2 tablespoons melted butter
Salt

Spread pecans on baking pan. Pour butter over top and toss to coat evenly. Bake at 250° for 25 to 30 minutes or until hot and slightly browned, stirring occasionally. Remove from oven and sprinkle generously with salt. Cool. Shake in colander to remove excess salt. Makes 2 cups.

CHUTNEY-SHRIMP KABOBS   CHILL

1-1$^1/_2$ pounds medium shrimp, cooked
1 cup mayonnaise
1 tablespoon finely minced onion
2 tablespoons chutney
1 teaspoon lemon juice
$^1/_2$ teaspoon curry powder

Combine last 5 ingredients until blended. Cover and chill until serving time. Place shrimp on toothpicks and serve with dip.
TIP: For Shrimp-Pineapple Kabobs, alternate pineapple chunks with shrimp on toothpicks.

OLIVE STUFFED CELERY   CHILL

Celery stalks
1 (8-ounce) package cream cheese, softened
1 teaspoon Worcestershire sauce
$^1/_4$ cup finely chopped ripe olives
$^1/_4$ cup finely chopped pecans

Wash celery stalks, trim and set aside. Combine remaining ingredients, stirring until blended. Fill celery stalks with mixture. Cover and chill. Cut in 2-inch pieces and arrange on serving plate.

NACHOS

MICROWAVE OR OVEN

Large size plain or taco flavored tortilla corn chips
1 (10¹/₂-ounce) can Fritos Jalapeño Bean Dip
Grated Cheddar cheese

Mound about a teaspoon of bean dip on each tortilla corn chip. Top with grated cheese. Place on paper plate and bake in microwave oven approximately 30 seconds. Or place on baking sheet and bake at 350° until cheese is melted. Serve hot.
TIP: Do not prepare ahead of time. The bean mixture tends to soften the corn chips and make them tough instead of crisp.

QUESADILLAS

OVEN

8 (8-inch) flour tortillas
3 cups (12-ounces) Monteray Jack cheese, grated
2 cups (8-ounces) Cheddar cheese, grated
Sliced black olives (optional)
Chopped green onion (optional)
Diced tomatoes (optional)

Place tortillas on ungreased baking sheet; bake at 400° for 1 to 1¹/₂ minutes. Don't let them crisp. Remove from oven and sprinkle four with grated cheese and, if desired, some of the optional ingredients. Top with remaining tortillas. Return to oven and bake until cheese is melted, 3 to 4 minutes.
TIP: Cut in wedges and serve with salsa or guacamole.

LINDA'S GUACAMOLE

The lime juice adds a delicious flavor and prevents the guacamole from turning brown.

2 ripe avocados
1 clove garlic, minced
Juice of ¹/₂ lime
Dash of Tabasco
1 small tomato, diced
Salt and pepper to taste

Peel and slice avocados. In a small bowl combine avocado slices, minced garlic, lime juice, and Tabasco; mash with fork until blended. Add tomato and salt and pepper to taste. Makes about 2 cups.
TIP: Serve with nachos, quesadillas, or tacos.

CLAM DIP

> 1 (8-ounce) package cream cheese, softened
> 1 (6-ounce) can minced clams, save juice
> 1 small garlic clove, minced
> 1/2 teaspoon lemon juice
> 1/4 teaspoon Worcestershire sauce
> Salt to taste

Combine cream cheese and clams. Stir in just enough juice to make a nice consistency for dipping. Add remaining ingredients and mix thoroughly. Serve or cover and chill. Serve with chips. Makes about 1 cup.

DILL DIP   CHILL

A favorite dip served with fresh chilled vegetables such as carrot sticks, cherry tomatoes, raw cauliflower, celery, cucumber sticks, and green pepper.

> 2/3 cup mayonnaise
> 2/3 cup sour cream
> 1 teaspoon dry minced onion
> 1 teaspoon dill weed
> 1 teaspoon Beau Monde seasoning (Spice Island)

Combine ingredients until blended. Cover and chill several hours or overnight to blend flavors. Remove from refrigerator just prior to serving. Makes $1^1/3$ cups.

SHRIMP DIP   MICROWAVE

> 1 can cream of shrimp soup
> 1 (8-ounce) package cream cheese
> 1 tablespoon lemon juice
> 1 tablespoon sherry

Put soup and cream cheese in small bowl. Cover and cook 3 to 4 minutes in microwave oven. Remove from oven and stir with fork until blended. Add lemon juice and sherry; blend. Cook 1 to 2 minutes more; stir. Serve hot with crackers, chips or raw vegetables. Makes 2 cups.

CHILLI DIP   TOP OF STOVE

> 1 (16-ounce) can chili con carne
> 1 (8-ounce) package cream cheese, cubed

Heat chili con carne in small saucepan. Add cubed cheese; stir until heated through and melted. Serve with assorted chips. Makes 2 cups.

HOT BACON-TOMATO DIP   TOP OF STOVE

Your guests will want the recipe for this one.

> **6 slices bacon, cooked crisp, crumbled**
> **1 can tomato soup**
> **1 (10-ounce) package frozen Stouffer's Welsh Rarebit**
> **1/4 teaspoon dried parsley**
> **1/4 teaspoon oregano**

In medium saucepan, combine all ingredients; cook until heated through.
Place in chafing dish and keep hot. Serve with corn chips.
TIP: To make ahead, combine ingredients in saucepan and heat just
before serving.

CHIHUAHUA DIP   TOP OF STOVE
                                          OVEN

Nice for a crowd. Serve with large tortilla chips.

> **1 pound well-seasoned sausage**
> **1 (16-ounce) can refried beans**
> **1 (4-ounce) can chopped green chilies**
> **2 cups (8-ounces) Monteray Jack cheese, grated**

In large skillet, crumble sausage and brown. Drain off all fat. Spread
refried beans in ungreased shallow 2-quart baking dish. Layer with
sausage, chilies and then cheese. Bake at 350° for 15 to 20 minutes or
until heated through. Makes 6 servings.

KIM'S ARTICHOKE DIP   OVEN

A family favorite.

> **1 (16-ounce) can artichoke hearts, drained and coarsely**
> **chopped**
> **1 (4-ounce) can chopped green chilies**
> **1 cup mayonnaise**
> **1 cup grated Parmesan cheese**

Combine ingredients and pour into 1 1/2-quart baking dish. Bake at 350°
for 20 to 30 minutes or until heated through. Serve warm with crackers.
TIP: If desired, this may be heated in saucepan on top of stove. Serve in
scooped out bread bowl.

HEAVENLY FRUIT DIP   CHILL

In about 3 minutes you can mix this and have it chilling in the refrigerator. Serve as a dip with fresh fruit or as a dressing over fruit salad. Yummy!

> 1 (3³/₄-ounce) package instant vanilla pudding mix
> 2¹/₂ cups half and half
> 1 tablespoon sugar
> ¹/₂ teaspoon rum extract
> ¹/₂ teaspoon vanilla extract

Combine ingredients in small mixing bowl; beat with rotary beater or lowest speed of mixer for about 2 minutes. Cover and chill several hours or overnight. Makes about 3 cups.

POTATO SKINS   OVEN

> Large potatoes (do not peel)
> Melted butter
> Salt and pepper
> Grated Cheddar cheese

Cut strips from potatoes about 2 to 4 inches long, and about 1 to 1¹/₂-inches wide, leaving a little potato on the skin. Place on cookie sheet and brush with melted butter. Bake at 375° for 10 minutes. Brush with additional butter and bake about 5 minutes more or until potato is tender and skin is crisp. Sprinkle lightly with salt and pepper. Sprinkle grated cheese over top. Return to oven to melt cheese. Serve hot.
TIP: Serve with your favorite condiments: sour cream, bacon bits, chives, taco meat, etc.

SAUSAGE STUFFED MUSHROOMS   OVEN

Allow 2 to 3 mushrooms per person.

> Large mushrooms
> Italian sausage
> Grated Parmesan cheese

Wipe mushrooms with damp cloth. Remove stems and hollow out center making room for the sausage. Fill each mushroom with sausage until mounded and rather compact. Place on baking sheet and sprinkle lightly with Parmesan. Bake at 350° for 25 to 30 minutes or until sausage is done. Serve hot.

EASY PARTY PUNCH   CHILL

A punch recipe that is kind to your budget. Great for picnics, weddings, showers, birthday parties, etc.

> **1 package cherry Kool-Aid**
> **1 package raspberry Kool-Aid**
> **2 cups sugar**
> **2 quarts water**
> **1 (46-ounce) can unsweetened pineapple juice**
> **2 quarts ginger ale (or to taste)**

Combine first 5 ingredients; chill. When ready to serve, pour mixture into punch bowl; stir in ginger ale. Makes 50 punch cup servings.

CRANBERRY PUNCH   CHILL

> **2 (46-ounce) cans unsweetened pineapple juice**
> **$^1/_2$ cup fresh lemon juice**
> **2 cups cranberry juice**
> **1 cup sugar**
> **2 quarts ginger ale**

Combine first 4 ingredients and chill. When ready to serve, stir in ginger ale. Makes 40 punch cup servings.

GOLDEN PUNCH   CHILL

> **1 (46-ounce) can apricot nectar**
> **1 (1 pint 2-ounce) can pineapple juice**
> **1 (6-ounce) can frozen lemonade, thawed**
> **1 (12-ounce) can frozen orange juice, thawed**
> **$1^1/_2$ quarts lemon-lime pop or ginger ale**

Combine first 4 ingredients and chill. When ready to serve, stir in pop or ginger ale. Makes 30 punch cup servings.

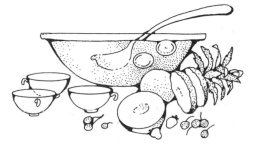

7-UP PUNCH

This recipe makes a beautiful green punch for weddings, St. Patrick's Day, Christmas or any special occasion. For White Wedding Punch, use vanilla ice cream and 7-Up, leaving small bits of ice cream for each punch cup.

2 quarts lime sherbet
3 quarts 7-Up, chilled

Spoon sherbet into a large punch bowl; pour in 7-Up to taste. Stir carefully until most of the sherbet has dissolved and punch is a colorful green. Makes 36 punch cup servings.

ICE CREAM PUNCH

You don't see milk in many punch recipes, but this one is very good.

2 small packages lemonade Kool-Aid
1 cup sugar
2 cups milk
1 quart ginger ale, chilled
1 pint vanilla ice cream

In small punch bowl, combine Kool-Aid and sugar. Add milk, stirring until mixed. Pour in ginger ale. Add ice cream by small spoonfuls. Serve right away. Makes 10 to 12 servings.

COMPANY GRAPEFRUIT DRINK

Grapefruit juice, chilled
Pineapple spears
Maraschino cherries

Pour grapefruit juice into glasses. Place a pineapple spear in each glass. Place toothpick in a maraschino cherry and insert into pineapple spear. TIP: Garnish with fresh mint leaves or watercress, if available.

REFRESHING APPLE DRINK

This is also good with cranberry juice and ginger ale.

Apple juice, chilled
Ginger ale, chilled

Mix equal parts apple juice and ginger ale. Pour over ice cubes and serve.

TWO-TONE JUICE COCKTAIL

> **2 cups pineapple juice, chilled**
> **2 cups tomato juice, chilled**
> **2 thin slices lemon, halved**
> **Parsley or mint sprigs**

In each 8-ounce parfait or cocktail glass, pour $^1/_2$ cup pineapple juice. Tip glass and slowly pour $^1/_2$ cup tomato juice down side of glass. Float a lemon slice on top and garnish with parsley or mint. Makes 4 servings. TIP: It is very important that you follow the directions carefully. You want a yellow layer and a red layer, but if you pour too quickly the colors will blend. Can be made up to an hour before serving.

CUP OF CHEER
TOP OF STOVE

> **1 cup sugar**
> **12 whole cloves**
> **2 (2-inch) pieces cinnamon sticks**
> **6 cups grapefruit juice**
> **3 cups orange juice**
> **4 cups apple cider**

In small saucepan, combine sugar, cloves and cinnamon sticks with $^1/_2$ cup water. Bring to a boil; reduce heat and simmer 20 minutes. Remove cloves and cinnamon sticks. In large pan or kettle, combine juices and apple cider; stir in sugar syrup. Heat gently until hot (do not boil). Serve hot. Makes 26 punch cup servings. TIP: Will keep up to 2 weeks in refrigerator. Remove amount needed; heat and serve.

HOT SPICED COFFEE
TOP OF STOVE

Satisfies your sweet tooth without adding calories.

> **4 cups water**
> **1 stick cinnamon**
> **1 teaspoon whole allspice**
> **2 small packages artificial sweetener**
> **Dash nutmeg**
> **1 tablespoon instant coffee**

Heat water in a large sauce pan. Add cinnamon, allspice, sweetener and nutmeg. Bring mixture to a full boil; remove from heat. Stir in coffee. Makes 4 servings.

DIABLO DRINK

A refreshing party drink on a hot summer day or evening.

> 1 (12-ounce) can limeade concentrate
> 1 juice can white rum
> Chilled 7-Up, approximately 2 liters, or to taste
> Crushed pineapple, drained
> Ice cubes

In large pitcher, combine limeade concentrate (do not dilute) and rum. Add 7-Up to taste. To each glass or punch cup, add a little crushed pineapple and ice cubes. Pour rum mixture over top.

FRESH SUNSHINE

Makes an elegant and refreshing drink

> 1 quart freshly squeezed orange juice, chilled
> 1 bottle champagne, chilled

Combine orange juice and champagne and pour into stemmed glasses. Makes 8 to 10 servings.

SUN TEA   SUNNY DAY

This tea is very easy to make, especially for a crowd. It doesn't have that bitter taste and doesn't turn cloudy in the refrigerator.

> 1 gallon cold water
> 7 tea bags

Fill gallon glass jar with the cold water. Add tea bags; put lid on. Place outside in sun and leave several hours or until of desired strength. Makes 1 gallon.

LEMON JULIUS

> 1 (6-ounce) can frozen lemonade concentrate
> 1 (6-ounce) can frozen orange juice concentrate
> 4 cups water
> 2 cups vanilla ice cream

Combine ingredients in blender; blend on medium speed until mixed and foamy. If blender is too small to hold all the ingredients, make half the recipe at a time and combine the two mixes. Make 7 $^1/_2$ cups.

LINDA'S ORANGE JULIUS

Almost as good as the original.

> 1 (6-ounce) can frozen orange juice concentrate
> 1 teaspoon vanilla extract
> 1 cup milk
> 1 cup water
> 1/2 cup sugar
> 6 ice cubes

Place ingredients in blender and blend until thoroughly mixed and ice is crushed. Serve right away. Makes 3 to 4 servings.

EASY EGG NOG   CHILL

> 1 (3³/₄-ounce) package instant vanilla pudding mix
> 2 eggs, beaten
> 1/3 cup sugar
> 1 teaspoon vanilla extract
> 6 cups milk
> Nutmeg

Using mixer on medium speed, combine pudding mix, eggs, sugar and vanilla. Gradually add milk, beating until thoroughly blended. Chill until ready to serve. Stir; pour into glasses and sprinkle with nutmeg. Makes 6 to 8 servings.

LEMONADE MIX

Stock up on lemons when they are on sale.

> **2 cups sugar**
> **1 cup water**
> **1¹/₂ cups fresh lemon juice, strained (about 6 lemons)**

Combine sugar and water in medium saucepan. Cook just until sugar dissolves, stirring frequently. Cool slightly. Pour lemon juice into quart container; add syrup. Stir to mix. Store in refrigerator until ready to use. Stir before using. Pour ¹/₄ cup mix into a 10-ounce glass. Add ice cubes and fill glass with cold water. Makes 1 quart concentrate.
TIP: For pink lemonade, add 1 tablespoon cranberry juice in 10-ounce glass of lemonade.

HOT BUTTERED RUM

> **1 pound light brown sugar**
> **1 pound butter, room temperature (do not substitute)**
> **1 quart vanilla ice cream (use a good brand), softened**
> **Dry white rum**

Combine brown sugar and butter in a large mixer bowl; beat until smooth. Add ice cream; beat until well mixed. Store in covered container in freezer. Remove from freezer when ready to serve. For each cup desired, add 1 heaping tablespoon batter to cup; fill cup with hot water and add 2 teaspoons rum (or to taste). Stir to melt batter. Serve hot.
TIP: The amount of batter and rum used depends on size of cups and individual tastes. Experiment to find what you like. Return remaining batter to freezer. Batter will keep several months and is convenient for drop in guests, especially during the winter holidays.

INSTANT HOT CHOCOLATE MIX

> **2 cups instant nonfat dry milk**
> **1 cup sugar**
> **¹/₄ cup cocoa**
> **¹/₂ teaspoon salt**

Sift ingredients together; store in covered container. Use approximately 3 tablespoons dry mix to 1 cup hot water.
TIP: Use hot tap water for children and they can drink it right away. Not expensive. Great for camping and boating.

WHITE BREAD   Oven

> $^1/_2$ cup hot water (105° to 115°)
> $^1/_3$ cup honey
> 3 packages dry yeast
> 3 cups hot tap water
> 1 tablespoon salt
> 8 to $8^1/_2$ cups flour

Combine the $^1/_2$ cup water and honey in a small bowl. Add yeast and stir slightly. Let stand about 10 minutes or until foamy and doubled in size. In large bowl, combine the 3 cups water, salt and 5 cups of the flour. Dough will still be quite sticky. Place on floured bread board and knead about 10 minutes or until dough is elastic. Add more flour as needed, dough should not be sticky. Place dough in a large greased bowl, turning to coat. Cover and let rise until doubled. Punch down dough. Divide for desired size pans filling pans half full. Cover and let rise until doubled in size. Bake at 350° for 30 to 45 minutes or until golden brown and bread sounds hollow when thumped. If desired, brush with butter or margarine. Remove from pans and let cool. Makes about 6 small loaves or 4 large loaves.
TIP: The larger the pan size, the longer it takes to bake. You can also shape into desired size rolls. The recipe calls for a lot of yeast, but is a help to the busy cook. The dough will rise much faster and the results are very good.

ENGLISH MUFFIN BREAD   Oven

> 1 package dry yeast
> 1 teaspoon salt
> 1 tablespoon sugar
> $1^1/_2$ teaspoons oil
> 5 cups flour
> Yellow cornmeal

In a large bowl, combine all the ingredients except the cornmeal. Stir in 2 cups hot tap water and mix thoroughly. Tightly cover bowl and let stand at room temperature at least 6 hours or overnight. The dough may double and fall, but that is okay.Butter two 7x3-inch loaf pans. Sprinkle lightly with the cornmeal, turning to coat evenly. Shake out excess. Punch dough down; divide in half. Shape into a loaf as best you can (dough is sticky) and place in pans. Cover and let rise until double, about 1 $^1/_2$ hours. This can vary depending on how warm your kitchen is. Bake at 350° for 60 minutes or until golden brown and bread tests done. Remove from pans and cool on rack.

EASY BATTER BREAD

OVEN

> 1 package dry yeast
> 1¼ cups water (105° to 115°)
> 2 tablespoons honey
> 2 tablespoons butter
> 1 teaspoon salt
> 3 cups flour

Combine yeast, water and honey in small bowl; stir slightly. Let stand until doubled in size, about 10 minutes. In large bowl, combine yeast mixture, butter, salt and 2 cups of the flour. If using mixer, beat on low speed until blended. Beat at medium speed for about 1 minute. Stir in remaining flour with wooden spoon. Cover and let rise in warm place, about 1 hour or until doubled in size. Stir batter down; spoon into greased 9x5-inch loaf pan. Cover and let rise in warm place, about 45 minutes or until doubled in size. Bake at 375° for 35 to 45 minutes or until browned and bread sounds hollow when tapped. Remove from pan and cool on rack. Makes 1 loaf.
Variations:
    RYE: Mix with 2 cups white flour, then add ¹/₂ cup white flour and 1 cup rye flour.
    WHOLE WHEAT: Mix with 1 ¹/₂ cups white flour and ¹/₂ cup whole wheat flour, then add 1 cup whole wheat flour.
    EGG: Use only ¹/₂ cup water with the yeast. Add 3 eggs along with the first 2 cups of flour.
    CHEESE: Add 1 cup (4-ounces) grated Cheddar Cheese along with the remaining cup flour.
TIP: This is exceptionally easy and quick if using a food processor.

EASY DINNER ROLLS

OVEN

My mother told me about this recipe. Different, delicious and very easy to prepare.

> 1 (9-ounce) box yellow Jiffy cake mix
> 1 package dry yeast
> ¹/₂ teaspoon salt
> 1¹/₄ cups hot tap water
> 2¹/₂-3 cups flour

Combine cake mix, yeast and salt. Add water to make a soft dough. (Dough will be quite sticky.) Cover; let rise until double, 1 to 1¹/₂ hours. Stir down dough; spoon onto a well-floured surface. Gently turn dough a couple times to lightly coat with flour. Shape into desired size rolls and place on greased baking sheets. Or shape into balls and place in greased muffin tins. Cover and let rise until double, about 1 hour. Bake at 400° for 10 to 15 minutes or until golden. Makes 15 to 18 rolls.

CRESCENT ROLLS   OVEN

> 2 packages dry yeast
> $^1/_2$ cup sugar
> 1 teaspoon salt
> 6-6$^1/_2$ cups flour
> 3 eggs, beaten slightly
> 1 cup melted butter

Dissolve yeast in 1 cup warm water (105° to 115°). Add sugar, salt and 1$^1/_2$ cups flour, stirring well. Add eggs, butter and remaining flour. Knead until smooth and elastic, about 10 minutes. Place dough in greased bowl, turning to coat. Cover and let rise in warm place about 1 hour or until doubled in size. Punch down; divide into 4 equal parts. Roll each part into a $^1/_4$-inch thick circle; cut into 12 wedges. Roll up for crescent, starting at wide end. Place on baking sheet; cover and let rise about 45 minutes or until double in size. Bake at 400° for 12 to 15 minutes or until golden. Makes 48 rolls.

REFRIGERATOR ROLLS   OVEN

You will find this recipe convenient when you have a busy week, but still want delicious homemade rolls for a special dinner. Dough can be made ahead and refrigerated overnight.

> 2 packages dry yeast
> 3 eggs, beaten lightly
> $^1/_2$ cup shortening
> $^1/_2$ cup sugar
> 1$^1/_2$ teaspoons salt
> 4$^1/_2$ cups flour

Combine yeast and 1 teaspoon of the sugar with $^1/_4$ cup water (105° to 115°). Set aside for 10 minutes to soften. Combine eggs, shortening, remaining sugar, salt and 2$^1/_2$ cups flour with 1 cup water. Beat by hand or with mixer until smooth. Add enough remaining flour to make a soft dough. Cover and let rise until doubled in size, about 1 to 1$^1/_2$ hours. Punch down dough. (At this point you can shape into rolls, let rise and then bake or you can refrigerate dough.) If refrigerated, remove about 3 hours before baking. Shape into desired size rolls. Place on baking sheet and let rise until doubled in size, about 2 hours. Bake at 400° for 12 to 15 minutes or until lightly browned. Makes about 18 to 20 rolls.

QUICK PECAN ROLLS   OVEN

> $^1/_2$ cup firmly packed brown sugar
> $^1/_2$ cup butter, melted
> 36 to 48 pecan halves (depending on size)
> Cinnamon
> 2 cups Bisquick mix
> $^1/_2$ cup cold water

Place 2 teaspoons brown sugar and 2 teaspoons melted butter in each of 12 muffin cups; stir to blend. Place 3 to 4 pecan halves in cups rounded side down. Sprinkle lightly with cinnamon. Combine Bisquick mix and water until soft dough forms, beating about 20 strokes. Spoon into muffin cups. Bake at 450° for 8 to 10 minutes; watch carefully so they don't burn. Invert pan on waxed paper leaving pan over rolls for a minute. Makes 12 rolls.
TIP: Best served hot, but almost as good cold. To substitute, use coarsely chopped walnuts for the pecan halves.

HOBO BREAD   TOP OF STOVE
                                                        OVEN

A moist, not too sweet bread. Allowing time for raisins to soak in boiling water at least 6 hours produces a more flavorful loaf of bread.

> 1 cup raisins
> 1 cup sugar
> 2 teaspoons baking soda
> 2 cups flour
> 2 tablespoons oil
> $^3/_4$ cup coarsely chopped walnuts

Bring 2 cups water to a boil. Turn off heat; add raisins. Cover; let stand at least 6 hours or overnight. In large mixing bowl, combine sugar, baking soda and flour. Add oil, walnuts and raisins with liquid. Stir just enough to moisten dry ingredients. Spoon into one greased and floured 9x5x3-inch loaf pan or two 7x3-inch loaf pans, filling about half full. Bake at 325° for 45 to 60 minutes or until browned and toothpick inserted in center comes out clean. Place pans on rack and let cool 5 minutes. Carefully run a thin knife around edges; remove from pans and let cool on rack.
TIP: Will keep better if stored in refrigerator. Can freeze.

BANANA BREAD   OVEN

>   1 cup butter or margarine, softened
>   2 cups sugar
>   2 cups mashed very ripe bananas
>   4 eggs, well beaten
>   2 teaspoons baking soda
>   2¼ cups flour

In large mixer bowl, cream the butter and sugar. Add bananas and eggs. Combine baking soda and flour. Add to banana mixture; stirring just enough to moisten the flour. Pour batter into 2 greased 9x5x3-inch loaf pans. Bake at 350° for 50 to 55 minutes or until bread tests done. Run knife around edge and turn out immediately. Cool on wire rack. Makes 2 loaves.

CHEESE SUPPER BREAD   OVEN

>   1½ cups Bisquick mix
>   1 egg
>   ¼ cup milk
>   1 cup (4-ounces) grated Cheddar cheese
>   1 teaspoon poppy seeds
>   2 tablespoons butter, melted

Combine Bisquick, egg, milk and ½ cup of the cheese; stir just until moistened. The dough will be stiff but sticky. With floured hands, pat dough evenly onto bottom of greased 9-inch pie pan. Sprinkle with poppy seeds and pour butter over top. Bake at 400° for 20 to 25 minutes or until lightly browned. Cut into wedges and serve hot. Makes 6 servings.
TIP: A definite cheese flavor. Best served fresh from the oven, but can be reheated.

GARLIC BREAD   OVEN

An all-time favorite.

>   1 loaf French bread
>   ½ cup butter
>   1-2 small garlic cloves, minced

Cut bread in slices or in half lengthwise. Place on ungreased baking sheet. Combine butter and garlic, mixing well. Spread on bread. Bake at 350° about 10 minutes or until lightly toasted.
TIP: If a softer bread is desired, wrap in foil and bake.

ORANGE BREAD

$^1/_2$ cup butter or margarine, softened
1$^1/_4$ cups sugar, divided
2 eggs
2 oranges
2 teaspoons baking powder
2 cups flour

Cream together butter, 1 cup of the sugar, and 1 egg. Beat in second egg. Squeeze juice from 1 orange and add water to measure $^1/_2$ cup. Grate rind from the orange and add to butter mixture along with the juice. (Mixture will look curdled.) Combine flour and baking powder. Add to above mixture, stirring just until moistened. Pour into greased 9x5x3-inch loaf pan. Bake at 350° for 55 to 60 minutes or until bread tests done. Meanwhile, squeeze juice from second orange and combine with remaining sugar in small saucepan. Bring to a simmer and heat until sugar is dissolved. Pour over hot bread. Let stand 10 minutes. Remove from pan and let cool on rack.
TIP: Bread slices easier the second day.

POPPY SEED FRENCH BREAD

Don't plan on leftovers with this recipe.

1 large loaf unsliced French bread
1 cup butter, melted
1 teaspoon poppy seeds
$^1/_4$ teaspoon garlic powder
$^1/_2$ teaspoon paprika

Trim crust from top and sides off bread. Slice lengthwise down the center, being careful to cut down to the bottom crust, but not through it. Cut across bread in $^1/_2$-inch slices, again being careful not to cut through the bottom crust. Combine remaining ingredients. Brush mixture over top and sides of bread and between the slices (depending on the size of the bread, you may not need all the butter mixture). Wrap bread in foil and set aside until just before serving. When ready to bake, fold foil down on all sides; place on baking sheet. Bake at 400° for 12 to 15 minutes or until golden brown. Serve on plate or basket and have guests pull off pieces of bread to eat. They will want to eat the bottom crust too, it is that good.
TIP: Can reheat in the oven, but not the microwave.

BLUEBERRY DROP BISCUITS   Oven

   1 cup flour
   $^1/_2$ teaspoon salt
   $1^1/_2$ teaspoons baking powder
   2 tablespoons butter
   $^1/_2$ cup milk
   $^1/_2$ cup fresh blueberries

Combine flour, salt and baking powder. Work in the butter with fork
or pastry blender. Add milk, stirring just to moisten. Carefully fold in
blueberries. Drop by tablespoon onto greased baking sheet. Bake at
375° for 12 to 14 minutes or until lightly browned. Makes 12 biscuits.

CRUNCHY BISCUIT TREATS   Oven

When in a hurry, these can't be beat.

   2 tablespoons butter or margarine, melted
   $^1/_3$ cup grated Parmesan cheese
   1 (10-ounce) package canned refrigerated biscuits

Pour butter into 9-inch pie plate. Sprinkle Parmesan evenly over the
butter. Arrange biscuits on top. Bake at 450° for 10 to 12 minutes or until
golden brown. Invert on serving plate.

SHORTCAKE BISCUITS   Oven

*Serve hot with lots of butter and jam or let cool and use as shortcake with fresh peaches
or strawberries.*

   1 cup whipping cream
   $^2/_3$ cup sugar
   $^3/_4$ teaspoon salt
   4 teaspoons baking powder
   2 cups flour

Whip cream until thickened. Combine remaining ingredients, stirring
to blend. Stir in whipped cream. You may have to get in there with your
hands to thoroughly mix in all the dry ingredients. Turn out on floured
surface and knead a couple of times to make a smooth dough. Pat to
$^1/_2$-inch thickness. Cut with $2^3/_8$-inch biscuit cutter. Place on ungreased
baking sheet. Bake at 425° for 10 to 12 minutes or until lightly browned.
If biscuits tend to get too brown on the bottom, you may have to raise
the oven rack. Makes 10 biscuits.
VARIATION: Pat dough into a $^1/_2$-inch thick circle and cut into 8 pie-
shaped wedges.

BAKING POWDER BISCUITS   OVEN

    2 cups flour
    3 teaspoons baking powder
    1 teaspoon salt
    $^1/_4$ cup shortening
    $^3/_4$ cup milk

Sift the flour, baking powder and salt together. Cut in shortening with
fork or pastry blender. Add milk and stir until flour is moistened. Turn
out on lightly floured board and knead about 20 times. Roll out or pat
to $^1/_2$-inch thickness. Cut with biscuit cutter and place on ungreased
baking sheet. Bake at 450° for 8 to 10 minutes or until lightly browned.
Makes 12 biscuits.

SALLY LUNN MUFFINS   OVEN

A wonderfully light, not too sweet muffin, that goes with almost any type of meal.

    $^1/_2$ cup butter or margarine, softened
    $^1/_3$ cup sugar
    1 egg
    3 teaspoons baking powder
    1$^1/_2$ cups flour
    $^3/_4$ cup milk

In mixer bowl, cream butter and sugar until thoroughly blended. Add
egg and mix well. Combine baking powder and flour. Add to the
creamed mixture alternately with the milk, starting and ending with
the flour. Spoon into greased muffin tins filling three-fourths full. Bake
at 400° for 18 to 20 minutes or until tests done. Remove from tins and
place on rack. Best served right away. Makes 12 large muffins.

WHOLE WHEAT MUFFINS   OVEN

    2 cups whole wheat flour
    $^1/_2$ cup sugar
    3$^1/_2$ teaspoons baking powder
    1 egg, slightly beaten
    3 tablespoons butter or margarine, melted
    1$^1/_2$ cups milk

In large mixing bowl, combine first 3 ingredients. Combine remaining
ingredients; add to dry mixture. Stir just until flour is moistened. Pour
into greased muffin tins, filling three-fourths full. Bake at 375° for 25 to
30 minutes or until done. Makes 12 muffins.

BRAN MUFFINS

A delicious bran muffin "without" sugar.

> **2 cups milk**
> **2 cups All-Bran cereal**
> **$^1/_4$ cup butter or margarine, softened**
> **2 eggs**
> **5 teaspoons baking powder**
> **2 cups flour**

Pour milk over All-Bran. Let stand until soft (about 5 minutes). Cream butter in mixer bowl. Add eggs and beat until smooth. Add bran mixture. Combine baking powder and flour. Add to bran mixture, stirring just enough to moisten the flour. Spoon into greased muffin tins, filling almost full. Bake at 375° for 25 to 30 minutes or until tests done. Makes 12 large muffins.

QUICK BLUEBERRY MUFFINS

A baking mix comes in handy for these quick and easy muffins.

> **2 cups Bisquick**
> **$^1/_4$ cup sugar**
> **1 cup sour cream**
> **2 eggs, beaten lightly**
> **$^1/_2$ cup chopped walnuts or pecans**
> **1 cup blueberries**

In medium bowl, combine Bisquick and sugar. Combine sour cream and eggs. Add to flour mixture, stirring just enough to barely moisten. Gently fold in nuts and blueberries. Put in greased muffin pan filling three-fourths full. Bake at 425° for 20 to 25 minutes or until tests done. Remove from pan and place on rack. Makes 12 muffins.

POPOVERS

> **1 cup flour**
> **$^1/_2$ teaspoon salt**
> **1 cup milk**
> **2 eggs**

Combine ingredients in small bowl; mix with hand mixer just until smooth. Pour into greased muffin tins or custard cups. Bake at 425° for 35 to 40 minutes or until golden. Serve immediately. Makes 8 popovers. VARIATION: Add $^1/_4$ cup grated sharp Cheddar cheese or 2 tablespoons finely chopped pecans and 1 teaspoon finely grated lemon rind.

CORNBREAD

CHILL
OVEN

An old favorite. Serve hot with plenty of honey and butter.

> **1 cup yellow cornmeal**
> **¹/₂ teaspoon salt**
> **2 tablespoons sugar**
> **2 tablespoons flour**
> **2 tablespoons shortening**
> **2 eggs, separated**

Combine first 4 ingredients. Bring 1 cup water to a boil and pour over top. Add shortening and stir until mixture is moistened and no lumps remain. Let cool in refrigerator while beating egg whites. Beat egg whites until stiff but not dry. Remove mixture from refrigerator; stir in the egg yolks to blend. Fold in the beaten egg whites. Pour into greased muffin tins, filling three-fourths full. Bake at 400° for 15 to 20 minutes or until golden. Makes 6 to 8 muffins.

LEMON SCONES

OVEN

Butter is all you need on these scones. They are wonderful served with a meal or with a cup of coffee. Best eaten hot out of the oven.

> **¹/₃ cup sugar**
> **¹/₂ teaspoon salt**
> **1 tablespoon baking powder**
> **2 cups flour**
> **1 tablespoon freshly grated lemon peel**
> **1¹/₄ cups whipping cream**

Combine first 5 ingredients in mixing bowl; mix well. Stir in whipping cream, mixing just until moistened. Turn out onto lightly floured board. Knead 6 to 8 times or until dough is smooth. Pat dough into an 8 ¹/₂-inch circle about ¹/₂-inch thick. Cut dough into quarters; cut each quarter into 3 triangles. Place triangles on ungreased baking sheet 2-inches apart. Bake at 425° for 10 to 12 minutes or until light golden brown. Makes 12 scones.

BASIC CREPES

This versatile crepe is good for many things, such as pancakes, main dishes, and desserts.

> **3 eggs, well-beaten**
> **1 cup milk**
> **1 tablespoon sugar**
> **$^1/_4$ teaspoon salt**
> **$^3/_4$ cup flour**

Beat together the eggs and milk. Add remaining ingredients and beat with mixer until smooth. Pour about 2 tablespoons batter into a buttered 8-inch skillet that has been preheated. Working quickly, rotate pan to spread batter evenly over the bottom. When cooked (this takes just a minute) turn crepe and cook other side. Turn out on dish and leave flat or roll up. Repeat, lightly buttering pan for each crepe. Makes about 16 crepes, depending on size of pan used.
TIP: Crepes can be made ahead and can be frozen.

CREAM PUFFS

> **$^1/_2$ cup butter**
> **1 cup water**
> **1 cup flour**
> **4 eggs**

In medium saucepan, bring butter and water to rolling boil. Add flour and stir vigorously over low heat until mixture forms a ball, about 1 minute. Remove from heat. Add eggs, one at a time, beating thoroughly. Drop from spoon onto ungreased baking sheet, about 3 inches apart, making desired sized cream puffs. Bake at 400°. For large puffs bake 45 to 50 minutes; for small puffs bake 30 minutes or until puffed, lightly browned and dry. Allow to cool. Cut off tops; remove soft dough and fill with desired filling. Makes 10 to 12 large or 35 to 40 small puffs.
TIP: Leave whole and frost with powdered sugar glaze. Or fill with whipped cream, pudding or ice cream. Tiny cream puffs can also be filled with assorted meat fillings and served as appetizers.

KRISTINA KRINGLER

TOP OF STOVE
OVEN

Have some friends over and serve fresh fruit with Heavenly Fruit Dip and Kristina Kringler. They'll love it and you won't have spent all day in the kitchen.

> 1 cup butter, chilled, plus 2 tablespoons butter, softened
> 2 cups flour, divided
> 2 teaspoons almond extract, divided
> 3 eggs
> 1¹/₂ cups sifted powdered sugar
> Chopped walnuts or pecans

With 2 knives or a pastry blender, cut ¹/₂ cup of the butter into 1 cup of the flour. Sprinkle 2 tablespoons water evenly over mixture; lightly mix with a fork. Form into a ball; divide in half. On ungreased baking sheet, pat each half into a strip, about 12x3-inches, allowing about 3 inches between the strips.

In medium saucepan, bring ¹/₂ cup butter and 1 cup water to a full boil. Remove from heat; quickly stir in 1 teaspoon almond extract and the remaining 1 cup flour. Return pan, over low heat, and stir until mixture forms a ball; this takes about a minute. Remove from heat. Add eggs; beat vigorously until smooth. Spread half of mixture evenly over each strip completely covering the top. Bake at 350° for 35 to 45 minutes or until lightly browned. Remove from baking sheet and cool on rack.

Combine remaining 2 tablespoons butter with powdered sugar, 1 teaspoon almond extract and 1 tablespoon water. Beat until smooth. It may be necessary to add more powdered sugar or water to make a nice consistency for spreading. Spread strips with frosting and sprinkle with nuts. Makes about 12 servings.
TIP: This is best eaten same day made.

CINNAMON TWISTS

OVEN

> 1 (12-ounce) package canned refrigerator biscuits
> Butter, softened
> ¹/₃ cup sugar
> 1 teaspoon cinnamon
> ¹/₂ cup sifted powdered sugar
> Water

Separate biscuits; flatten each one into a 4-inch round. Spread each circle with about a teaspoon of butter. Combine sugar and cinnamon and sprinkle evenly over circles. Cut circle in half; place butter sides together and twist. Place on cookie sheet. Bake at 400° for 10 to 12 minutes or until golden brown. Combine powdered sugar and water to make a glaze. Drizzle over cinnamon twists while still warm. Makes 10.

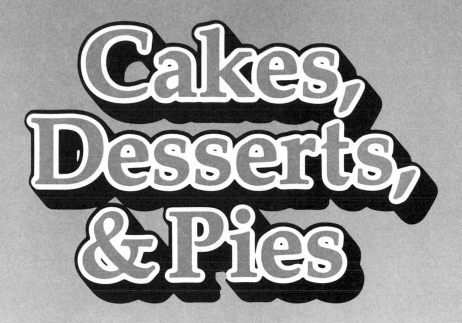

Cakes, Desserts, & Pies

DATE NUT CAKE

A wonderfully moist date cake that can be served plain, with ice cream or frosted with a Buttercream Frosting.

> **8 ounces dates, finely chopped**
> **$^1/_2$ cup butter or margarine**
> **1 cup firmly packed light brown sugar**
> **1 teaspoon baking soda**
> **$1^1/_2$ cups flour**
> **1 cup chopped walnuts**

Combine dates and butter with $^3/_4$ cup hot tap water. Let stand 10 minutes. Meanwhile, combine sugar, baking soda and flour. Add to date mixture. Stir in walnuts. Pour into greased and floured 8-inch baking pan. Bake at 375° for 30 to 40 minutes or until cake tests done. Let cool on rack. Makes 9 servings.

SOUR CREAM CHOCOLATE CAKE

I think you will like this recipe. It makes a dense moist cake and slices beautifully.

> **3 (1-ounce) squares semi-sweet chocolate**
> **2 tablespoons butter or margarine**
> **3 eggs, separated**
> **$1^1/_2$ cups sugar, divided**
> **1 cup sour cream**
> **1 cup flour**

Melt chocolate in top of double boiler (or microwave). Stir in butter until melted. Beat egg whites until soft peaks form. While continuing to beat egg whites, slowly add 1 cup of the sugar and beat until stiff but not dry. Set aside. In mixer bowl, beat egg yolks and the remaining $^1/_2$ cup sugar until thoroughly mixed. Add chocolate and sour cream. Alternately fold in flour and egg whites, about a third at a time, mixing only until smooth. Pour into greased and floured 9x13-inch baking pan. Bake at 325° for 30 to 35 minutes. Cake should start to shrink from edge of pan. Cool. Frost with a thin layer of your favorite chocolate frosting.

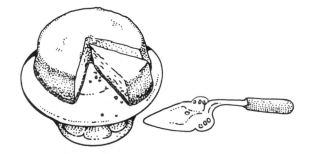

STRAWBERRY REFRIGERATOR CAKE

OVEN
CHILL

1 (18^{1}/$_{2}$-ounce) package white cake mix
1^{1}/$_{3}$ cups water
2 egg whites
1 (3-ounce) package strawberry jello
1 cup boiling water
1 (8-ounce) container Cool Whip, thawed

Mix cake according to package directions, using the 1 ^{1}/$_{3}$ cups water and egg whites. Pour into greased 9x13-inch pan. Bake at 350° for 30 to 35 minutes or until cake tests done. Remove cake from oven; pierce all over with long-tined fork. Dissolve jello in boiling water and pour over cake. Cover and chill. Spread Cool Whip evenly over top of cake. Cut into squares and serve.
TIP: If desired, garnish with chopped walnuts or a fresh strawberry.

SPECIAL LUNCH BOX CAKE

OVEN

2 cups sugar, separated
2 teaspoons baking soda
2 cups flour
2 eggs, slightly beaten
1 (17-ounce) can fruit cocktail (do not drain)
^{3}/$_{4}$ cup coarsely chopped walnuts

In mixing bowl, combine 1^{1}/$_{2}$ cups of the sugar, baking soda and flour. Add eggs and undrained fruit cocktail. Mix well and pour into greased 9x13-inch baking pan. Sprinkle remaining ^{1}/$_{2}$ cup sugar evenly over top. Sprinkle nuts over sugar. Bake at 300° for 60 minutes or until cake tests done.

TRIPLE FUDGE CAKE

OVEN

1 (3-ounce) package regular chocolate pudding mix
2 cups milk
1 (18^{1}/$_{2}$-ounce) package devils food cake mix
^{1}/$_{2}$ cup semi-sweet chocolate chips
^{1}/$_{2}$ cup chopped walnuts

Prepare pudding mix with milk as directed on package. Remove from heat; blend dry cake mix into hot pudding. Mixture will be quite thick and spongy. Pour into greased and floured 9x13-inch pan. Sprinkle with chocolate chips and nuts. Bake at 350° for 30 to 35 minutes.
TIP: This is a heavy spongy type cake, but is great for eating out of hand and for sack lunches.

CHERRY CAKE SQUARES

    1 cup butter
    1¹/₂ cups sugar
    4 eggs
    1 teaspoon lemon extract
    2 cups flour
    1 (21-ounce) can cherry or blueberry pie filling

Cream butter and sugar in large mixer bowl until light and fluffy. Add eggs, one at a time, beating after each addition. Add lemon extract. Stir in flour. Pour batter into greased 15x10x1-inch jelly roll pan. Mark off 20 squares. Put 1 tablespoon pie filling in center of each square. Bake at 350° for 45 minutes or until done. Cool and cut into squares. Makes 20 servings.
TIP: If desired, sprinkle with sifted powdered sugar while still warm.
VARIATION: For a quick and easy coffee cake, prepare the cake batter and pour half of the batter into a greased Bundt cake pan. Sprinkle with ¹/₄ cup cinnamon sugar (¹/₄ cup sugar, ¹/₂ teaspoon cinnamon). Pour remaining batter over top. You may have to increase baking time.

CREAM CHEESE CUPCAKES

    3 (8-ounce) packages cream cheese, softened
    1¹/₄ cups sugar
    5 eggs
    3 tablespoons vanilla extract
    1 (21-ounce) can cherry or blueberry pie filling
    1 cup sour cream

In mixer bowl, combine cream cheese and 1 cup of the sugar. Add eggs and 2 tablespoons of the vanilla. Beat until thoroughly mixed, 3 to 4 minutes. Line muffin tins with paper cupcake liners. Fill three-fourths full and bake at 300° for 30 to 40 minutes. Remove from oven and let cool 5 minutes (centers will drop while cooling). Combine sour cream, the remaining ¹/₄ cup sugar and remaining 1 tablespoon vanilla extract. Fill center of cupcakes with 1 tablespoon sour cream mixture. Put a teaspoonful of pie filling on top. Return to oven and bake 5 minutes. Let cool in refrigerator.
TIP: The amount of vanilla extract is correct, but if using a good brand of pure vanilla you may wish to decrease this amount.

BROWNIE CUPCAKES

Brownie fans will enjoy these.

> 1 cup butter or margarine
> $^2/_3$ cup semi-sweet chocolate chips
> $1^3/_4$ cups sugar
> 4 eggs
> 1 teaspoon vanilla extract
> 1 cup flour

Melt butter and chocolate chips in microwave oven or in saucepan, over low heat. Stir in sugar; mix well. Add eggs, vanilla and flour. Stir until blended and smooth. Pour into cupcake liners, filling three-fourths full. Bake at 350° for 25 to 30 minutes or until done. Makes 16 large cupcakes. TIP: For variety, add $1^1/_4$ cups coarsely chopped walnuts to batter or sprinkle top of each cupcake with walnuts before baking.

CHERRY CUPCAKES

> 1 cup butter or margarine
> $1^1/_2$ cups sugar
> 4 eggs
> 1 teaspoon vanilla extract
> 2 cups flour
> 1 (21-ounce) can cherry pie filling (or blueberry, apple)

In large mixer bowl, cream butter and sugar until light and fluffy. Add eggs, one at a time, beating well after each addition. Add vanilla. Add flour and mix until blended and smooth. Place paper liners in muffin tins and fill a little over half full. Make a slight indentation in center, fill with pie filling using about 3 cherries per cupcake. Bake at 350° for 30 to 35 minutes or until light golden. Makes 22 cupcakes. TIP: If desired, when cool, drizzle with a small amount of glaze: Add a little water to powdered sugar until you get the desired consistency.

POUND CAKE

> 1 pound butter
> 1 (16-ounce) box powdered sugar, sifted
> 6 eggs
> $1^1/_2$ teaspoons vanilla extract
> 3 cups sifted cake flour

Cream butter and powdered sugar in large mixer bowl. Add eggs, one at a time, and beat well. Stir in vanilla and flour. Pour into greased and floured angel food cake pan. Bake at 350° for about $1^1/_4$ hours. Cool. (While still slightly warm sift additional powdered sugar over top.)

WHIPPED BUTTER FROSTING

> 5 tablespoons flour
> 1 cup milk
> 1 cup sugar
> 1 cup butter, softened
> 1 teaspoon vanilla extract

Combine flour and milk in small saucepan (do not use aluminum). Cook over low heat until quite thick, stirring constantly. Remove from heat; let cool. Cream together sugar, butter and vanilla. Add cooled mixture and beat, beat, beat. When finished, frosting looks like thick whipped cream.
TIP: Frosting or frosted cake must be refrigerated.

FAVORITE CHOCOLATE FROSTING

> $^1/_4$ cup milk
> $^1/_4$ cup butter
> 1 (6-ounce) package semi-sweet chocolate chips
> 1 teaspoon vanilla extract
> $2^1/_2$ cups sifted powdered sugar

Combine milk and butter in small sauce pan. Bring to a boil; remove from heat. Stir in chocolate chips until melted and smooth. Place chocolate mixture, vanilla and powdered sugar in mixing bowl. Beat until of spreading consistency. If necessary, thin with a few drops of milk.
TIP: If desired, stir in $^1/_2$ cup chopped walnuts and spread on 9x13-inch chocolate cake. Work quickly before frosting loses its shine.

PENUCHE FROSTING

> $^1/_3$ cup butter or margarine
> $^1/_2$ cup firmly packed light brown sugar
> 3 tablespoons milk
> $^1/_4$ teaspoon vanilla extract
> 2 cups sifted powdered sugar

Melt butter in small saucepan. Add brown sugar. Cook over medium heat, stirring constantly, until sugar melts. Add milk; bring to a boil. Remove from heat; let cool 10 minutes. Stir in vanilla and powdered sugar. Beat until blended and smooth. Add additional sugar if necessary. Makes about 1 cup.

CREAM CHEESE FROSTING

> 1 (16-ounce) box powdered sugar, sifted
> $^1/_2$ cup butter, softened
> 1 (8-ounce) package cream cheese, softened
> 1 teaspoon vanilla extract

Combine ingredients in large mixing bowl; mix until smooth. Spread on cake or cupcakes.
TIP: This is a delicious frosting for Carrot Cake. If desired, add $^1/_2$ cup crushed pineapple, drained. Frost cake and sprinkle top with chopped nuts. Store in refrigerator.

BUTTERCREAM FROSTING

> $^1/_4$ cup butter or margarine, softened
> 3 cups sifted powdered sugar
> 1 teaspoon vanilla extract
> 3 to 4 tablespoons milk

In small mixer bowl, cream butter. Add sugar, vanilla and 3 table-spoons milk. Beat until creamy and thick enough to spread. It may be necessary to add more milk or more powdered sugar to get consistency desired. Makes enough frosting for a 9x13-inch cake.
TIP: Frosting can be changed by substituting different liquids for the milk such as lemon or orange juice, coffee, chocolate, etc.

CONFECTIONER'S GLAZE

> 1 cup sifted powdered sugar
> 1 tablespoon hot water
> $1^1/_2$ teaspoons light corn syrup
> $^1/_4$ teaspoon vanilla extract

Combine ingredients in small mixing bowl; stir until blended and smooth. Consistency should be thin, but not run off cake. Add more powdered sugar or water, if necessary. Makes about 1/2 cup.

RICE CHEX DESSERT

This recipe is worth the price of the cookbook.

2^1/$_2$ cups crushed Rice Chex cereal
1 cup firmly packed light brown sugar
1 cup cashews, split
^{1}/$_2$ cup butter, melted
1 cup Angel Flake coconut
^{1}/$_2$ gallon vanilla ice cream, softened

Combine first 5 ingredients; mix thoroughly. Spread half of mixture evenly in buttered 9x13-inch baking dish; pat down. Spread ice cream evenly over top. Sprinkle remaining cereal mixture over ice cream; pat lightly. Cover and freeze. When ready to serve, remove from freezer and cut into squares. Makes 12 to15 servings.
TIP: When in season, top each serving with a fresh strawberry.

APPLE CRISP

Reminds me of hot apple pie, but a lot easier to make.

4 cups sliced apples
1 teaspoon cinnamon
^{1}/$_2$ teaspoon salt
^{3}/$_4$ cup flour
1 cup sugar
^{1}/$_3$ cup cold butter

Place apple slices in buttered 10x7-inch baking dish; sprinkle with cinnamon and salt. Pour ^{1}/$_4$ cup water over apples. Combine flour and sugar in small mixing bowl. With fork or pastry blender cut in butter. Sprinkle mixture evenly over apples. Bake at 350° for 40 minutes or until light golden and apples are tender. Makes 6 servings.
TIP: If desired, sprinkle apples with ^{1}/$_3$ cup chopped walnuts. Serve warm with vanilla ice cream.

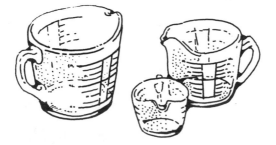

HEAVENLY RICE PUDDING   TOP OF STOVE

An old time favorite rich and creamy dessert.

> **3 cups half and half**
> **$1/4$ cup sugar**
> **2 cups cooked rice (not Minute Rice)**
> **2 tablespoons butter or margarine**
> **1 teaspoon vanilla extract**

Combine all the ingredients in a medium size heavy saucepan. Simmer 20 to 30 minutes, or until thick. Pour into 4 to 5 small custard cups. Serve warm or cold. Makes 4 to 5 servings.
TIP: If storing in refrigerator, cover with plastic wrap.

CHOCOLATE DATE DESSERT   TOP OF STOVE
                                                CHILL

A wonderful way to use up that last cup of dates.

> **1 cup chopped dates**
> **2 cups small marshmallows**
> **$1/2$ cup coarsely chopped pecans**
> **16 Oreo cookies**
> **5 tablespoons butter or margarine, melted**
> **1 cup whipping cream**

In small saucepan, combine dates and $3/4$ cup water. Bring to a boil, reduce heat, simmer 3 minutes. Remove from heat. Add marshmallows and stir to blend. Let cool. Add pecans. Crush Oreos in blender or food processor. Remove 1 tablespoon and set aside for garnish. Add melted butter to crumbs. Press into 9-inch square dish. Spread date mixture on top. Whip cream and spread over date mixture. Sprinkle top with reserved crumbs. Chill several hours or overnight. Makes 9 servings.

CREME DE MENTHE PARFAITS

> **Vanilla ice cream**
> **Cream De Menthe**

Layer ice cream and Creme De Menthe in parfait glasses, ending with Creme De Menthe.
TIP: If desired, garnish with whipped cream, finely chopped nuts and a maraschino cherry.

FANTASTIC CHEESECAKE

The ultimate dessert.

> $^1/_3$ cup graham cracker crumbs
> 3 (8-ounce) packages cream cheese, softened
> 4 eggs
> $1^3/_4$ cups sour cream, divided
> 1 cup sugar, plus 1/4 sugar
> 4 tablespoons fresh lemon juice

Heavily butter a 9-inch springform pan. Put crumbs in pan and rotate to cover bottom and sides. Discard loose crumbs. In mixer bowl, cream the cream cheese until smooth. Add eggs, one at a time, and mix well. Add $^3/_4$ cup of the sour cream, 1 cup of sugar and 2 tablespoons of the lemon juice. Mix until blended and smooth. Pour into springform pan. Bake at 350° for 35 to 40 minutes or until just firm (do not overbake). Meanwhile combine the 1 cup sour cream, $^1/_4$ cup sugar, and 2 tablespoons lemon juice. When done, remove cheesecake from oven and carefully spoon sour cream mixture over top. Return to oven and bake 5 minutes. Let cool on rack. Chill. Makes 12 servings.
TIP: For a delicious topping try Cherries Jubilee, sweetened strawberries, or a blueberry sauce with almond.

CREME BRULEÉ

A popular dessert in many of your nicer restaurants—now you can make your own.

> 2 cups whipping cream
> $^1/_2$ cup sugar plus some for top
> 4 egg yolks
> 1 tablespoon vanilla extract

Pour cream into medium saucepan and heat over low heat until bubbles begin to form around edge of pan. Do not boil. In mixer bowl, beat egg yolks and sugar together until thick and light yellow, 2 to 3 minutes. Beating constantly, slowly add cream to egg mixture, adding a tablespoon at a time at first, then when egg mixture is thin, pour remaining cream in a steady stream. Add vanilla. Pour into shallow custard cups or a quiche pan. Place in baking pan. Pour about an inch of boiling water into pan. Bake at 350° for 45 to 50 minutes or until custard has thickened. Remove from pan and chill at least 2 hours. Sprinkle top with a very thin layer of granulated sugar. Place under broiler and cook until sugar is melted and golden brown. Watch carefully, you don't want it to burn. Chill. Makes 4 to 5 servings.

BAKLAVA

The first time I made Baklava, the recipe was two pages long. This one is easier and just as moist and delicious.

> $4^1/_2$ cups walnuts, finely ground
> 3 cups sugar, separated
> $1/_2$ teaspoon cinnamon
> 1 pound box phyllo, thawed and at room temperature
> 1 pound butter, melted
> 1 tablespoon lemon juice

Combine walnuts, $1^1/_2$ cups of the sugar and cinnamon. Butter a 15x10-inch jelly roll pan. Unroll phyllo and place on flat surface. Cover with waxed paper or plastic. Then cover with a slightly damp towel. Phyllo must be kept covered at all times as it dries out quickly. Lay 1 sheet of phyllo in pan. You may have to fold one end over to fit pan. Brush with melted butter. Repeat layering until half of phyllo has been used. Spread nut mixture evenly over top. Repeat layering with remaining phyllo continuing to butter each layer. With a sharp knife, cut through layers of phyllo, cutting in a diamond shaped pattern, making cuts about $1^1/_2$ inches apart. Bake at 300° for 70 to 80 minutes or until golden brown.

    Meanwhile, in medium saucepan, combine $1^1/_2$ cups of water with the remaining $1^1/_2$ cup sugar and lemon juice. Bring to a boil, stirring frequently to dissolve sugar. Lower heat and simmer 20 minutes. Let cool slightly. Spoon syrup over Baklava. Let stand 3 to 4 hours to absorb syrup.

TIP: This makes a lot, but can also be frozen.

PISTACHIO DESSERT

> 50 Ritz crackers, crushed
> $1/_2$ cup butter or margarine, melted
> 1 quart vanilla ice cream, softened
> 1 cup milk
> 1 ($3^3/_4$-ounce) package instant pistachio pudding mix
> 1 (8-ounce) container Cool Whip, thawed

Combine cracker crumbs and butter. Pat evenly into unbuttered 9x13-inch baking dish. Bake at 350° for 10 to 15 minutes. Remove from oven and let cool. In mixer bowl, blend ice cream, milk and pudding mix. Pour over crust. Spread Cool Whip over top. Chill several hours or overnight. Makes 10 to 12 servings.

VARIATION: Sprinkle top with toasted coconut, crushed Heath candy bars, grated chocolate or chopped nuts.

CAROLYN'S PEANUT DELIGHT

1 (13^1/$_2$-ounce) package Nutter Butter Cookies, finely crushed
^{1}/$_4$ cup melted butter
^{1}/$_2$ gallon vanilla ice cream, softened
2 cups Spanish peanuts
1 (12-ounce) carton Cool Whip, thawed
Chocolate or Butterscotch sauce

Combine cookie crumbs and melted butter in mixing bowl; mix well. Spread evenly in buttered 9x13-inch dish. Using finger or a spatula, pat mixture evenly and firmly. Spread ice cream over top. Sprinkle with peanuts. Spread Cool Whip over peanuts. Cover and freeze. To serve, cut in squares and place on individual serving plates. Drizzle a small amount of sauce over top. Makes 12 servings.

CHERRY PARFAITS

1 cup whipping cream
3 tablespoons sugar
1 teaspoon vanilla extract
1 cup sour cream
1 (21-ounce) can cherry pie filling

Whip cream in small mixer bowl, adding sugar, and vanilla. Fold in sour cream. Alternate layers of whipped cream mixture and cherry pie filling in parfait glasses, beginning with a red layer and ending with a white layer. Chill until serving time. Makes 4 to 5 servings.
TIP: If desired, top with a single cherry or finely chopped nuts.

CROISSANT BREAD PUDDING

2^1/$_2$ cups half and half
6 eggs, beaten slightly
^{3}/$_4$ cup sugar, separated
^{1}/$_2$ teaspoon cinnamon
8 croissants (day old works best)
^{3}/$_4$ cup dark raisins

Combine half and half with the eggs. Combine ^{1}/$_2$ cup of the sugar with cinnamon; add to egg mixture. Pour into buttered 2-quart shallow baking dish. Tear croissants into bite-size pieces. You should have about 7 cups. Pour into custard, pressing down to cover. Sprinkle raisins over top. Sprinkle remaining ^{1}/$_4$ cup sugar over raisins. Bake at 350° for 40 to 45 minutes or until set. Serve warm with a little additional cream. Makes 6 servings.

CHERRIES JUBILEE

TOP OF STOVE

1 tablespoon sugar
1 tablespoon cornstarch
1 (16-ounce) can Bing cherries, pitted
$^1/_2$ teaspoon lemon juice
$^1/_4$ cup warm brandy
Vanilla ice cream

Combine sugar and cornstarch in chafing dish or saucepan. Slowly add liquid from canned cherries and stir to blend. Cook over low heat until thickened, stirring constantly. Add cherries and lemon juice; heat through. Pour brandy over top and carefully ignite. Serve over ice cream. Makes 4 servings.

TIP: This is such a popular dessert, I double the recipe for 4 people. Flame in front of your guests and they'll love it. For additional flavor, add 4 strips fresh orange peel to sugar, cornstarch and liquid mixture.

DUMP CAKE

OVEN

An old recipe, but still a favorite.

1 (20-ounce) can crushed pineapple with juice
1 (16-ounce) can cherry pie filling
1 (18$^1/_2$-ounce) package yellow cake mix
$^3/_4$ cup butter

Dump pineapple with juice into buttered 9x13-inch baking pan. Spread evenly. Dump cherry pie filling evenly over pineapple. Sprinkle cake mix over fruit. Slice butter very thin and distribute over top. Bake at 350° for 45 minutes or until golden. Makes 8 to 10 servings.

ICE CREAM BALLS

FREEZE

An easy dessert to be enjoyed year round.

Vanilla ice cream
Sliced almonds
Chocolate sauce

Scoop ice cream into balls. Quickly roll in almonds to coat. Cover and freeze. When ready to serve, place one ice cream ball per serving in a champagne glass or dessert dish. Warm chocolate sauce and pour over top. Use one ice cream ball per serving.

VARIATIONS: Use Angel Flake coconut or chopped pecans, walnuts or macadamia nuts. Serve with sweetened sliced strawberries, raspberries or peaches. Cherries Jubilee is delicious served over ice cream balls.

LEMON MOUSSE

Almost my favorite dessert.

1 envelope Knox gelatin
2 tablespoons cold water
$^1/_3$ cup fresh lemon juice
4 eggs
1 cup sugar
1 cup whipping cream, whipped

In very small saucepan or small metal cup, combine gelatin and water, stirring to mix well. Place over low heat and heat slowly until dissolved, stirring frequently to blend. When smooth and somewhat clear, remove from heat. Add lemon juice and set aside. Meanwhile, beat eggs with sugar until a light lemon color. Stir in gelatin. Reserve about $^3/_4$ cup of the whipped cream for garnish. Fold remaining whipped cream into lemon mixture. Pour into champagne or wine glasses or small custard cups. Chill until set. This will take about 3 hours. Garnish with whipped cream. Makes 5 to 6 servings.

CHOCOLATE MOUSSE

2 (1-ounce) squares sweet chocolate
3 (1-ounce) squares unsweetened chocolate
5 egg yolks (save 4 of the egg whites)
$^3/_4$ cup sugar
$^1/_2$ teaspoon vanilla extract
$1^1/_4$ cups whipping cream, whipped

Melt both chocolates in top of a double boiler over hot, but not boiling, water. Remove from heat and cool. Beat egg yolks with $^1/_2$ cup of the sugar until light and thick. Add the chocolate and vanilla. Beat egg whites until soft peaks form. Slowly add remaining $^1/_4$ cup sugar and beat until firm peaks form. Beat about $^1/_4$ cup of meringue into chocolate mixture. Fold in remaining meringue and whipped cream. Spoon into one large serving bowl or small individual serving cups. Chill. This is very rich, servings should be small. Makes 8 to 10 servings.

FRUIT LAYER DESSERT CHILL

1¼ cups crushed vanilla wafers
½ cup butter
1½ cups sifted powdered sugar
2 eggs
4 cups sliced fresh strawberries
1 cup whipping cream, whipped

Crush vanilla wafers and put in buttered 8x12-inch pan. (If desired, save some for sprinkling over top.) Cream butter and sugar well. Add eggs one at a time; mix thoroughly. Pour over crushed wafers. Arrange strawberries over top. Spread whipped cream over strawberries, spreading to edges to seal. sprinkle with reserved crumbs. Chill overnight. Makes 10 to12 servings.
VARIATION: Sprinkle finely chopped walnuts over top.

ICE CREAM CAKE FREEZE

When in their teens, this is the dessert my children wanted for their birthday cake. Just add candles to the top.

1½ packages Ladyfingers, split
1-1½ quarts chocolate ice cream, softened
1-1½ quarts vanilla ice cream, softened
10 Heath candy bars, coarsely crushed

Line sides and bottom of angel food cake tube pan with Ladyfingers, rounded side out. Half fill pan with chocolate ice cream. Sprinkle half of the crushed candy over top. Spread vanilla ice cream over candy; sprinkle with remaining crushed candy. Cover with foil and freeze. Makes 12 to 14 servings.
TIP: If you wish to make a smaller dessert, use half the ingredients and a 9x5-inch loaf pan lined with foil (so you can easily remove the dessert from the pan).

CANDIED BANANAS TOP OF STOVE

3 tablespoons butter
4 firm bananas, peeled, cut in half lengthwise and crosswise
3 tablespoons sugar

Melt butter in heavy skillet over low heat. Add bananas cut side down; cook until lightly browned. Sprinkle sugar over bananas and cook until glazed. Serve warm. Makes 4 servings.
TIP: Omit sugar and use as a side dish with pork or fried eggs.

ANGEL CAKE SURPRISE

1 Angel Food cake
3 cups whipping cream
$^1/_3$ cup sugar
4 cups fresh strawberries, sliced

Cut lid from cake, cutting horizontally about 1-inch from top. Remove center of cake, cutting down to within one inch of bottom of cake and leaving a one inch wall all around. Whip cream with sugar. Add berries to half of whipped cream. Fill cavity with strawberry filling and replace top. Frost cake with remaining whipped cream. Chill at least 3 hours. TIP: Garnish with fresh whole strawberries. To substitute, use fresh raspberries. You could also fill inside of cake with your choice of ice cream. Frost with sweetened whipped cream; freeze until ready to serve.

EASY PARTY CAKE

1 Angel Food cake
2 cups whipping cream
$^1/_4$ cup sugar
2 (10-ounce) boxes frozen strawberries, thawed

Whip cream, adding $^1/_4$ cup sugar or more to taste. Frost cake with whipped cream. To serve, cut cake and spoon strawberries over each serving. Makes 10 servings.

LEMON DELIGHT

An ideal light dessert that is cake and pudding all in one dish.

3 eggs, separated
Juice and grated peel of 2 large lemons
2 tablespoons butter, melted
$^1/_2$ cup flour
$1^1/_2$ cups milk
$1^1/_2$ cups sugar, divided

Combine egg yolks, lemon juice, grated peel, butter, flour, milk and 1 cup of the sugar. Beat until smooth. Beat egg whites until soft peaks form. Add remaining $^1/_2$ cup sugar and beat until stiff but not dry. Gently fold into first mixture. Pour into ungreased shallow, 2-quart baking dish. Set in larger pan. Pour about 1 inch hot water into larger pan. Bake at 375° for 40 to 45 minutes or until set. Chill before serving. Makes 6 servings.

FROZEN LEMON VELVET   FREEZE

Joe, my son-in-law, likes this dessert almost as much as "cheesecake". Keep one in the freezer for spur-of-the-moment entertaining.

    1 cup plus 1 tablespoon crushed vanilla wafers
    $1/2$ cup fresh lemon juice
    $1^{1}/2$ cups sugar
    6 eggs, separated
    3 cups whipping cream

Line bottom of ungreased 9-inch springform pan with the 1 cup crumbs. In large mixer bowl, combine lemon juice and sugar. Add egg yolks and beat until thick. Whip cream and gently fold into lemon mixture. Beat egg whites until stiff but not dry. Fold into mixture until thoroughly combined. (I hope your mixing bowl is large because this makes a lot.) Pour into springform pan and mound as high as you can. Sprinkle with remaining 1 tablespoon crumbs. Freeze. When frozen, cover with foil and store in freezer. Makes 12 servings.
TIP: Unmold and cut desired number of servings. Place in refrigerator for about an hour to soften slightly. This is a beautiful dessert served with sweetened sliced strawberries poured over the top of each slice.

PEACH MELBA

    1 (16-ounce) can peach halves, drained
    1 pint vanilla ice cream
    $1/4$ cup raspberry preserves

Place one peach half in each of 4 small serving dishes. Fill center with a scoop of ice cream; top with 1 tablespoon preserves. Makes 4 servings.
TIP: To substitute, use frozen raspberries, thawed, for the preserves.

CHOCOLATE CUPS   TOP OF STOVE
                                              CHILL

    6 (1-ounce) squares semi-sweet chocolate
    2 tablespoons vegetable shortening

Put ingredients in top of double boiler and melt over hot, but not boiling, water. Stir to blend. With small brush, paint a layer of chocolate in paper muffin cups, painting the bottom and sides to about $1/8$ inch from top of cup. Chill or freeze until firm. Remove from refrigerator or freezer, one at a time, and carefully peel off paper. Keep chilled until ready to serve.
TIP: Number of cups made depends on size of muffin cups and thickness of chocolate layer (do not paint too thin). Fill with ice cream, or mousse type puddings. Garnish with a crisp sugar cookie.

FROZEN FUDGESICLES

1 (4-ounce) package instant chocolate pudding mix
2 cups milk
$^1/_4$ cup sugar
1 cup canned evaporated milk

Combine pudding and the 2 cups milk in large mixer bowl. Beat 2 minutes. Stir in sugar and canned milk. Pour into popsicle molds and freeze. Makes about 18 Fudgesicles.

CHOCOLATE SEA SHELLS

This is a wonderful way to serve ice cream. Sea shells can usually be found in kitchen and import stores.

6 (1-ounce) squares semi-sweet chocolate
4 large scallop sea shells
Foil squares

Melt chocolate in top of double boiler or in microwave. Stir until smooth. Cover outside of each shell tightly with foil, tucking about one inch of foil underneath. Pressing carefully on the foil, smooth out as many wrinkles as possible to form the shape of the shell. With a small brush, narrow spatula or knife, spread a thick layer of chocolate over foil, spreading to within $^1/_4$ inch of edge of shell. Be careful not to let any of the chocolate run underneath. Place shells in refrigerator and chill until firm, about 20 minutes. Remove foil from shell. Carefully peel foil from chocolate. Try not to touch chocolate with your hands any more than you have to; the warmth from your hands can soften the chocolate. Cover; chill until ready to serve. Makes 4 shells.
TIP: Can be filled with ice cream, sherbet, mousse, etc.

DEVONSHIRE CREAM AND BERRIES

1 (8-ounce) package cream cheese, softened
$^1/_2$ cup sifted powdered sugar
$^1/_3$ cup whipping cream
1 teaspoon vanilla extract
$1^1/_2$ teaspoons Grand Marnier liqueur
Fresh strawberries

In mixer bowl, whip cream cheese and powdered sugar until thoroughly blended and smooth. Add whipping cream, vanilla, and Grand Marnier; whip until light. Serve with berries. If not using right away, cover and chill. Makes $1^1/_2$ cups.

PIE CRUST

> 2 cups flour
> 1 teaspoon salt
> $^3/_4$ cup shortening
> $^1/_4$ cup ice water

Combine flour and salt in mixing bowl. With fork or pastry blender, cut in shortening until uniform, about the size of peas. Sprinkle with water, a tablespoon at a time, and toss with fork. Stir gently, just until dough forms a ball. Divide into 2 equal parts; place on lightly floured surface and roll to $^1/_8$-inch thickness. Gently ease into pan to avoid stretching. Makes 2 single crusts.

STEVE'S PERFECT PIE CRUST   CHILL

> 4 cups flour
> 1 tablespoon sugar
> 2 teaspoons salt
> 1$^3/_4$ cups shortening (do not substitute)
> 1 tablespoon cider or white vinegar
> 1 large egg

Combine flour, sugar and salt in a mixing bowl. Cut in shortening with fork or pastry blender. Combine vinegar and egg with $^1/_2$ cup cold water; add to flour mixture. Stir until moistened and a dough is formed. Divide dough into 5 equal parts; shape each into a round flat patty ready for rolling. Wrap in waxed paper; chill at least 30 minutes. Place on lightly floured board; roll $^1/_8$-inch thick and 2 inches larger than inverted pie pan. Makes 5 single crusts.
TIP: Dough can be refrigerated up to 3 days or can be frozen. Steve was a lifesaver one Thanksgiving when he made the pumpkin pies for me. The crust turned out flaky and the filling was delicious.

PRESS IN PAN PIE CRUST

> 1 cup flour
> 2 tablespoons sugar
> 6 tablespoons butter
> 1 egg yolk

Combine flour, sugar and butter in small bowl. Stir with fork until blended. Add egg yolk and mix with wooden spoon; working mixture into a smooth ball. Press pastry evenly into bottom and up sides of 9-inch pie pan. Makes 1 crust.

BUTTER CRUNCH CRUST OVEN

$1^1/_2$ cups flour
$^1/_4$ cup plus 1 tablespoon firmly packed light brown sugar
$^1/_2$ cup plus 1 tablespoon butter
$^1/_2$ cup finely chopped nuts

Combine ingredients in mixing bowl; mix with fork or pastry blender until crumbly. Spread evenly in 9x13-inch baking pan. Bake at 450° for 15 minutes. While still warm, stir with fork; press into desired size pan. TIP: If desired, reserve some for topping. If using as a base for a 9x13-inch dessert, remove from oven, stir and press evenly into same pan.

GRAHAM CRACKER CRUST OVEN

$1^1/_4$ cups graham cracker crumbs
$^1/_4$ cup sugar
$^1/_3$ cup melted butter

Combine ingredients and press into bottom and sides of 9-inch pie pan. Bake at 350° for 10 minutes. Cool.

PRETZEL PIE CRUST OVEN

A wonderfully versatile pie crust that is compatible with a variety of fillings.

$^3/_4$ cup butter or margarine, melted
$2^2/_3$ cups crushed pretzels
3 tablespoons sugar

Combine ingredients and pat into two 9-inch pie pans or one 9x13-inch pan. Bake at 350° for 10 minutes. Cool.

MERINGUE SHELL OVEN

3 egg whites, room temperature
$^1/_8$ teaspoon salt
$^1/_2$ teaspoon cream of tartar
1 cup sugar
$^1/_2$ teaspoon vanilla extract

In large mixer bowl, add egg whites, salt and cream of tartar; beat until soft peaks form. At low speed, gradually add sugar and beat until all sugar has been dissolved. Add vanilla and beat until very stiff and glossy. Spread on bottom and sides of greased 9-inch pie pan. Bake at 300° for 40 minutes or until shell feels dry on the outside. Cool thoroughly on wire rack. Fill with desired filling.

APPLE CRUMB PIE   OVEN

> 1 (9-inch) unbaked pie shell
> 6-7 tart apples, peeled and sliced
> 1 cup sugar
> 1 teaspoon cinnamon
> $3/4$ cup flour
> $1/3$ cup butter

Arrange apple slices in pie shell. Combine $1/2$ cup sugar and cinnamon; sprinkle over apples. Combine remaining sugar and flour in small bowl. With fork or pastry blender, cut in butter until crumbly. Sprinkle evenly over apples. Bake at 400° for 40 minutes or until apples are tender. Makes 6 servings.
TIP: Although not a tart apple, the Golden Delicious makes a very good pie.

SOUR CREAM APPLE PIE   OVEN

Apple pie is always a favorite and this one is just a little different.

> $3/4$ cup sugar, plus 2 tablespoons
> 3 tablespoons flour
> 1 cup sour cream
> 3 cups coarsely chopped apples (3 medium)
> 1 (9-inch) unbaked pie shell
> 1 teaspoon cinnamon

Combine the $3/4$ cup sugar, flour and sour cream; mix well. Add chopped apples. Pour into pie crust. Mix the remaining 2 tablespoons sugar with the cinnamon. Sprinkle evenly over apple mixture. Bake at 400° for 15 minutes. Reduce heat to 350° and bake 25 to 30 minutes or until apples are tender. Cool. Makes 6 servings.

RAISIN-NUT PIE   OVEN

> 2 eggs, separated
> $1/2$ cup butter or margarine, melted
> 1 cup sugar
> $1/2$ cup raisins
> $1/2$ cup chopped pecans
> 1 (9-inch) unbaked pie shell

Combine egg yolks with next 4 ingredients. Beat egg whites until stiff but not dry. Fold into mixture. Pour into pie shell. Bake at 300° for 40 to 45 minutes or until lightly browned. Cool. Makes 6 servings.

LINDA'S CHERRY PIE

> **Pastry for 2-crust pie**
> **1¹/₄ cups sugar, divided**
> **5 tablespoons cornstarch**
> **¹/₄ teaspoon cinnamon**
> **2 (16-ounce) cans tart cherries (pitted)**
> **1 tablespoon butter**

In small saucepan, combine ³/₄ cup of the sugar, cornstarch and cinnamon until blended. Drain cherries; reserve one cup juice. Stir cherry juice into sugar mixture. Cook over low heat, stirring frequently, until mixture thickens. Add remaining ¹/₂ cup sugar. Stir in cherries. Line a 9-inch pie pan with pastry; add pie filling. Dot with butter. Add top crust (or a lattice); cut slits in top. Bake at 425° for 45 to 55 minutes or until golden.
TIP: For a deeper red, add a few drops red food coloring. For a nice change, add ¹/₂ teaspoon almond extract with remaining ¹/₂ cup sugar.

FRESH STRAWBERRY PIE

One of the best strawberry pies and always a favorite among guests.

> **1 (9-inch) baked pie shell**
> **1 cup sugar**
> **1 cup water, divided**
> **3 tablespoons cornstarch**
> **3 tablespoons strawberry jello**
> **3-4 cups fresh whole strawberries**

Put sugar in small saucepan. Combine ¹/₄ cup of the water with the cornstarch, stirring until smooth. Add cornstarch mixture and the remaining ³/₄ cup water to saucepan; mix well. Cook over medium low heat until thickened, stirring frequently. Stir in jello. Line pie shell with strawberries, pointed end up. Fill in where necessary with smaller berries. Pour sauce over top. Chill until set. Makes 6 servings.
TIP: Delicious topped with whipped cream.

CHOCOLATE MINT PIE

**1 (6-ounce) package semi-sweet chocolate chips
2 tablespoons butter or margarine, softened
2 tablespoons powdered sugar
$^1/_2$ gallon chocolate chip mint ice cream, softened**

Line a 9-inch pie pan by pressing a 12-inch square of heavy duty foil on bottom, sides and rim of pan. Sprinkle chocolate chips evenly over foil. Put in 250° oven for about 5 minutes or until chocolate is soft. Remove from oven. Add butter and stir until melted. Add powdered sugar. Spread mixture over bottom and sides of pan. Chill until firm, about 30 minutes. Carefully remove foil and return shell to pan. Fill with softened ice cream. Freeze. Makes 6 to 8 servings.
TIP: Chocolate shell can be filled with your choice of ice cream and fillings. One of my favorite is a layer of chocolate and vanilla ice cream with a layer of crushed Heath Candy bars in the middle and sprinkled on top. Another is a chilled lemon or chocolate filling. Garnish as desired.

AMAZING COCONUT PIE

An "Impossible Pie" that makes its own crust.

**3 eggs
$^1/_4$ cup butter or margarine, softened
$1^1/_2$ teaspoons vanilla extract
1 (14-ounce) can Eagle Brand sweetened condensed milk
$^1/_2$ cup Bisquick mix
1 cup Angel Flake coconut**

In blender or mixer, combine first 5 ingredients along with $1^1/_2$ cups water; mix well. Pour into a buttered deep dish 10-inch pie plate. Sprinkle coconut over top. Bake at 350° for 40 to 45 minutes or until mixture is set and knife inserted just off center comes out clean. Chill. Makes 6 servings.

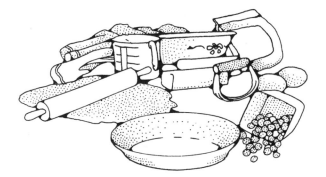

FROZEN LEMON PIE

3 eggs, separated
$^1/_2$ cup plus 2 tablespoons sugar
Juice of 1 lemon
1 cup whipping cream, whipped
Graham cracker crumbs, about $^1/_2$ cup

Beat egg whites until soft peaks form. Add the 2 tablespoons sugar and beat until stiff, but not dry. Set aside. Beat egg yolks, the $^1/_2$ cup sugar and lemon juice until thick and light in color. Gently combine the whipped cream, beaten egg whites and egg yolk mixture. Line bottom of a butttered 9-inch pan with a layer of graham cracker crumbs. Pour filling over top and sprinkle lightly with graham cracker crumbs. Freeze. Cover and freeze until ready to serve. Makes 6 to 8 servings. TIP: Can be taken directly from freezer and served. For Christmas, top with a red maraschino cherry and add a touch of green such as green maraschino leaves or holly leaves.

CREAMY LEMON MERINGUE PIE

A light lemon pie that is just right with a cup of coffee and good conversation.

4 eggs, separated
1 cup sugar, divided
$^1/_4$ cup lemon juice
2 teaspoons grated lemon rind
1 tablespoon water
1 (9-inch) baked pie shell

In top of double boiler, beat egg yolks and $^1/_2$ cup of the sugar until light yellow. Add lemon juice, grated rind and water. Place over boiling water and stir often with a wire whisk until thickened; about 4 to 6 minutes. Remove from heat and let cool, stirring occasionally. Meanwhile, beat egg whites until soft peaks form. Gradually add remaining $^1/_2$ cup sugar and beat until stiff but not dry. Fold half of meringue into lemon mixture. Pour into pie shell. Spread rest of meringue over top, making sure to seal all edges by completely covering the filling. Swirl to make high peaks. Bake at 425° until lightly browned, about 5 to 7 minutes. Chill for several hours before serving. Makes 6 servings.

CRUNCH PIE OVEN

    whites
    1 cup sugar
    1 teaspoon baking powder
    1 teaspoon vanilla extract
    1 cup crushed graham cracker crumbs
    1 cup chopped pecans

Beat egg whites until stiff. Combine sugar and baking powder; beat into egg whites. Add vanilla. Fold in graham cracker crumbs, then pecans. Pour into buttered 9-inch pie plate. Bake at 350° for 30 minutes or until done. Cool.
TIP: Very good served with vanilla ice cream or whipped cream.

DEEP DISH FRUIT PIE OVEN

This takes less than 5 minutes to prepare and you'll have it baking in the oven while you do something else.

    1/2 cup butter, melted
    1 cup Bisquick mix
    1 cup sugar
    1 cup milk
    1 quart fruit, drained (peaches, blackberries, etc.)

Pour butter into 10x6-inch shallow baking dish. Stir in Bisquick, sugar and milk. Pour fruit over top. Bake at 375° for 35 to 40 minutes or until golden brown. Makes 6 servings.
TIP: Very good served warm with vanilla ice cream.

QUICK GERMAN CHOCOLATE PIE TOP OF STOVE
FREEZE

    1 (9-inch) baked pie shell
    1 (4-ounce) package sweet chocolate
    1/3 cup milk, divided
    2 tablespoons sugar
    1 (3-ounce) package cream cheese, softened
    1 (8-ounce) container Cool Whip, thawed

In sauce pan, heat chocolate and 2 tablespoons of the milk, over low heat, until chocolate is melted and mixture is smooth. In small mixer bowl, beat sugar and cream cheese until smooth. Add remaining milk and the chocolate mixture; beat until smooth. Fold in Cool Whip. Spoon into pie shell. Freeze. Makes 6 servings.

DREAMSICLE PIE

This recipe reminds me of my childhood ,when a Dreamsicle ice cream bar tasted so good on a hot summer day.

1 (8¹/₂-ounce) package plain chocolate wafers
¹/₄ cup melted butter
1 quart vanilla ice cream, softened
1 quart orange sherbet, softened

Crush wafers in blender or food processor. Reserve 1 teaspoon for top. Add melted butter; mix to blend. Press into bottom and sides of a deep 9-inch pie pan. Spread half of vanilla ice cream over crust. Spread sherbet over ice cream. Spread remaining ice cream over sherbet. Sprinkle reserved crumbs over top. Cover and freeze. Makes 6 servings.

PEANUT BUTTER PIE

1 (8-ounce) package cream cheese, softened
1 cup creamy peanut butter
1 cup sugar
2 tablespoons butter, melted
1 cup whipping cream
1 (9-inch) baked pie crust

In mixer bowl, beat the cream cheese until smooth. Add peanut butter, sugar and butter; beat until smooth. Whip the cream and add to peanut butter mixture; mix well. Pour into pie shell. Chill until firm.
TIP: A graham cracker crust can be substituted for the pie crust.

LEMON ICE CREAM PIE

1¹/₂ pints vanilla ice cream
3 eggs
¹/₂ cup sugar
¹/₄ cup fresh lemon juice
1 cup whipping cream
¹/₄ cup finely chopped pecans

Soften ice cream slightly. Spoon into a foil-lined 9-inch pie pan; press to form a crust. Freeze. In small saucepan, beat 1 egg, 2 egg yolks, (save remaining 2 egg whites) sugar and lemon juice. Cook over low heat, stirring constantly, until thick. Remove from heat and cool. Beat egg whites until stiff, but not dry. Whip cream. Fold cream into lemon mixture. Fold in beaten egg whites. Pour into ice cream shell. Sprinkle with pecans. Freeze.
VARIATION: Omit pecans and serve with sweetened strawberries.

BUSY DAY PUMPKIN PIE

OVEN
CHILL

This is one of those recipes that is even better the second day.

>   1 (16-ounce) can pumpkin
>   1 (14-ounce) can Eagle Brand sweetened condensed milk
>   1 egg
>   1 teaspoon pumpkin pie spice
>   1 teaspoon cinnamon
>   1 (9-inch) unbaked pie shell

Combine first 5 ingredients and blend well. Pour into pie shell. Bake at 375° for 50 to 55 minutes or until knife inserted just off center comes out clean. Let cool, then place in refrigerator until ready to serve.

BANANA SPLIT PIE

FREEZE

>   1 (9-inch) baked pie shell
>   3 bananas, sliced
>   1 tablespoon lemon juice
>   1 pint strawberry ice cream, softened
>   1¹/₂ cups Cool Whip
>   Chocolate sauce

Sprinkle bananas with lemon juice, turning to coat. Arrange on bottom of pie shell. Spread ice cream over bananas. Spread Cool Whip over top. Freeze. Remove from freezer 20 minutes before serving. Cut and serve with chocolate sauce. Makes 6 servings.

DAIQUIRI PIES

CHILL

My daughter made these for Mother's Day one year. They make a delicious, not too heavy, dessert.

>   1 (8-ounce) package cream cheese, softened
>   1 (14-punce) can Eagle Brand sweetened condensed milk
>   1 (6-ounce) can limeade concentrate, thawed
>   ¹/₃ cup light rum
>   1 (4-ounce) container Cool Whip, thawed
>   2 baked 9-inch pie shells

In mixer bowl, beat cream cheese until light and fluffy. Add condensed milk and limeade, mix well. Add rum. Fold in Cool Whip. Pour into pie shells. Chill at least 4 hours. Makes 2 pies.

TIP: For a different combination, substitute Pretzel Pie Crust for the baked pie crusts. Or pour filling into dessert dishes and top with whipped cream and toasted coconut.

RAISIN CRUNCHIES

    1 (12-ounce) package semi-sweet chocolate chips
    $1/2$ teaspoon vanilla extract
    $1^{1}/2$ cups raisins
    $1/2$ cup peanuts
    1 cup Corn Flakes

Melt chocolate chips in top of double boiler, stirring until smooth. Remove from heat; stir in vanilla, raisins, peanuts and Corn Flakes. Drop by teaspoon onto waxed paper-lined cookie sheet. Chill until firm. Makes about 3 $1/2$ dozen.
TIP: If desired, spread mixture evenly into lightly buttered 9-inch square dish: chill; cut into squares.

EASY SUGAR COOKIES

    $1/2$ cup butter or margarine
    $1/2$ cup sugar
    1 teaspoon vanilla extract
    1 egg yolk (reserve white)
    1 cup flour

Combine ingredients in mixer bowl until blended. Shape into small balls and place on ungreased cookie sheet. Beat egg white slightly with fork. Dip fork in egg white and lightly press cookie. Sprinkle with additional sugar. Bake at 350° for 8 to 10 minutes. They should not brown but should be light in color. Makes 2 $1/2$ dozen.
TIP: This is a small recipe so double or triple, as desired.

JAN HAGEL COOKIES

    1 cup butter, softened
    1 cup sugar
    1 egg, separated
    2 cups flour
    $1/2$ teaspoon cinnamon
    $1/2$ cup finely chopped walnuts or pecans

Cream butter, sugar and egg yolk in mixer bowl. Combine flour and cinnamon; stir into creamed mixture. Pat evenly into greased 10x15-inch jelly roll pan. With fork, beat egg white with 1 tablespoon water; brush over dough. Sprinkle with nuts. Bake at 350° for 20 to 25 minutes or until golden brown. Cut into bars while hot. Makes about 5 dozen.
TIP: If desired, make drop cookies. Flatten slightly; brush with egg white glaze and sprinkle with nuts.

Raspberry Meringue Bars

Oven

$^3/_4$ cup shortening
$^1/_3$ cup sugar plus $^1/_2$ cup sugar
2 eggs, separated
$1^1/_2$ cups flour
1 cup raspberry preserves
1/3 cup finely chopped walnuts

Cream shortening and $^1/_3$ cup sugar in mixer bowl. Add egg yolks and mix thoroughly. Stir in flour. Pat mixture evenly into bottom of 9x13-inch pan. Bake at 350° for 15 minutes or until golden in color. Cool. Spread preserves evenly over crust. Beat egg whites until soft peaks form; gradually add the $^1/_2$ cup sugar and beat until stiff but not dry; spread over preserves. Sprinkle with nuts. Bake at 350° for 30 minutes. Makes 3 to 4 dozen.

Pecan Snowballs

Oven

1 cup butter
$^1/_4$ cup sugar
2 teaspoons vanilla extract
2 cups sifted flour
Small pecan halves (4-5 dozen)
Sifted powdered sugar

Mix butter, sugar, vanilla, and flour as for pie crust (cut in with fork or pastry blender). Pinch off small amount of dough and wrap around a pecan half, sealing to cover. Place on ungreased cookie sheet. Bake at 350° for 10 minutes or until light golden in color. While still hot, roll in powdered sugar. Let cool and roll again in powdered sugar. Makes 4 to 5 dozen.

Butterscotch Marshmallow Cookies

Top of Stove
Chill

1 cup peanut butter
$^1/_2$ cup butter or margarine
2 (6-ounce) packages butterscotch chips
4 cups colored or white miniature marshmallow

Melt peanut butter, butter and butterscotch chips in top of double boiler; stir to blend. Remove from heat and cool slightly. Gently stir in marshmallows. Pour into buttered 9-inch square dish. Chill. Cut into squares. Makes 3 dozen.

BUTTERSCOTCH DROP COOKIES

2 (6-ounce) packages butterscotch chips
$^1/_2$ cup creamy or chunky peanut butter
2 cups Corn Flakes

Melt butterscotch chips and peanut butter in top of double boiler; stir to blend. Remove from heat and gently stir in corn flakes to coat. Drop by teaspoon on waxed paper-lined cookie sheet. Chill until set. Makes 3 $^1/_2$ dozen.

SPRITZ

1$^1/_4$ cups butter, softened
1 cup sugar
2 eggs
2 teaspoons vanilla extract
$^1/_2$ teaspoon salt
3 cups flour

Cream butter and sugar until light and fluffy. Add eggs, one at a time, beating after each addition. Add vanilla extract. Stir in salt and flour. Chill if necessary. Press through cookie press onto ungreased cookie sheets. Bake at 375° for 8 to 10 minutes or until crisp, but not browned. Makes about 4 $^1/_2$ dozen.

FRENCH MADELEINES

These are absolutely delicious. They taste like crisp little butter cakes.

4 eggs
2 cups sugar
2 cups flour
1$^1/_2$ cups butter, melted
1 tablespoon vanilla extract
Sifted powdered sugar

Combine eggs and sugar in top of double boiler. Heat until lukewarm. Remove from heat and place mixture in mixer bowl. Beat until cooled. Add flour gradually, mixing well after each addition. Add melted butter and vanilla, mixing until smooth. Use special shell shaped Madeleine molds which have been greased and floured, or small 1$^1/_2$-inch greased and floured muffin tins. Fill molds two-thirds full. Bake at 425° for 8 to10 minutes or until just lightly browned around the edges. Remove from oven; let stand about a minute. Tap pan to release cakes; cool on rack. Makes 6 dozen.
TIP: Can freeze. Just before serving, sift powdered sugar lightly over top.. The amount of vanilla extract called for is correct.

SANDBAKKELS

1 cup butter, softened
1 cup sugar
1 egg, lightly beaten
1 teaspoon almond extract
2$^{1}/_{2}$-3 cups flour

Cream butter and sugar until light. Beat in egg. Add almond extract. Add enough flour to make a soft dough. Press a small amount of dough into tiny fluted metal molds, making sure dough is spread evenly, and not too thick. Place molds on cookie sheet and bake at 375° for 10 to 12 minutes or until a very light golden color. Do not allow to brown. Cool slightly; tap bottom of molds to release. Makes 6 to 8 dozen.
TIP: These little butter cookies are delicious as is or filled with your favorite lemon filling just before serving (garnish with a tiny dab of whipped cream).

CHRISTMAS HOLLY COOKIES

35 large marshmallows
$^{1}/_{2}$ cup butter or margarine
1 teaspoon vanilla extract
1$^{1}/_{2}$ teaspoons green food coloring (approx.)
4 cups Corn Flakes
Red hot candies (for decoration)

Melt marshmallows and butter in top of double boiler; stir to blend. Stir in vanilla extract and enough food coloring to make a dark green. Remove from heat and gently stir in corn flakes. Working quickly, drop by teaspoon onto waxed paper-lined cookie sheet. Decorate each cookie with 3 red hots for holly berries. Chill. Makes 3 dozen.
TIP: These make a colorful addition to a tray of assorted holiday cookies.

BUTTERSCOTCH CRUNCHIES

1 (6-ounce) package butterscotch chips
$^{1}/_{2}$ cup peanut butter
2 cups (3-ounce can) Chow Mein Noodles
1 cup miniature marshmallows

Melt butterscotch chips and peanut butter in top of double boiler; stir to blend. Remove from heat. Gently stir in noodles and marshmallows. Drop by teaspoon onto waxed paper-lined cookie sheets. Chill until set. Makes 3 dozen.

COCONUT MACAROONS

$^1/_2$ cup egg whites (about 4 eggs)
$^1/_4$ teaspoon salt
$^3/_4$ cup sugar
1 teaspoon vanilla extract
4 cups shredded coconut

In medium saucepan, over low heat, combine egg whites, salt and sugar. Heat until warm, but not hot — you don't want to cook the egg whites. Remove from heat and stir in vanilla and coconut. Drop into mounds, about the size of a walnut, onto greased baking sheet. Bake at 300° for 20 to 25 minutes or until macaroons start to lightly brown on the bottom and around the edges. Cool on rack. Makes about 36.
VARIATION: Add $^3/_4$ cup finely chopped dates and/or $^1/_2$ cup chopped walnuts.

MOSAIC COOKIES

I had to hide these in the freezer or my children would eat them all in one sitting.

1 (12-ounce) package semi-sweet chocolate chips
$^1/_2$ cup butter or margarine.
1 (10$^1/_2$-ounce) package colored miniature marshmallows
1 cup chopped walnuts
3$^1/_2$ cups Angel Flake coconut

In top of double boiler, melt together the chocolate chips and butter. Place marshmallows and nuts in large mixing bowl. Pour melted chocolate over top; stir carefully to coat. Chill about 15 minutes to make handling easier. Sprinkle coconut on bread board. Spoon one third of chocolate mixture in a log row (about 10 to 12 inches) on top of coconut. Roll in coconut, shaping to make a roll. Place on waxed paper or foil; wrap and twist ends. Repeat with remaining mixture. Chill until firm. Slice to serve. Makes about 7 dozen.

PEANUT BUTTER LOGS

1 (6-ounce) package semi-sweet chocolate chips
$^1/_3$ cup peanut butter
4 cups Cocoa Krispies

Melt chocolate chips in top of double boiler. Stir in peanut butter. Remove from heat. Gently stir in Cocoa Krispies. Press mixture into buttered 9-inch square pan. Cool; cut into bars. Makes 3 dozen.

EASY KID'S COOKIES

OVEN

    1 cup firmly packed light brown sugar
    1 cup butter or margarine, softened
    1 cup flour
    1 teaspoon baking soda
    2 cups quick cooking rolled oats

Cream sugar and butter in mixer bowl. Add flour and baking soda. Stir in oats. Roll into 1-inch balls. Place on ungreased baking sheet and press slightly. Bake at 350° for 8 to 10 minutes. Makes 4 dozen.

DATE NUT ROLLS

TOP OF STOVE

    $1/2$ cup butter or margarine
    1 (8-ounce) package dates, chopped
    1 cup sugar
    1 cup finely chopped walnuts
    1 teaspoon vanilla extract
    $1^1/2$ cups Rice Krispies cereal

Melt butter in medium saucepan. Stir in dates, sugar and nuts. Cook over low heat for 8 to 10 minutes or until thickened. Remove from heat; add vanilla and cereal. Shape into balls or small rolls. Makes 3 dozen. TIP: If desired, roll in Angel Flake coconut.

MIKE'S BABE RUTH BARS

TOP OF STOVE

When Mike had friends stay over, they always made these cookies and devoured every ont of them.

    1 cup sugar
    1 cup light corn syrup
    1 cup chunky peanut butter
    6 cups Special K cereal
    1 (6-ounce) package semi-sweet chocolate chips
    1 (6-ounce) package butterscotch chips

Combine sugar and corn syrup in 2-quart saucepan. Place over medium heat and bring to a boil, stirring occasionally. Remove from heat. Add peanut butter and mix well. Stir in cereal until evenly coated. Press mixture into a buttered 9x13-inch pan. Cool. Melt chips in top of double boiler; stir to blend thoroughly. Spread over cooled mixture. Cool; cut into bars. Makes about 4 dozen.

CARAMEL BROWNIE BARS

TOP OF STOVE
OVEN

44 vanilla caramels
$^2/_3$ cup canned evaporated milk, divided
1 (18$^1/_2$-ounce) package German chocolate cake mix (do not substitute)
1 cup chopped walnuts (not too coarse)
$^2/_3$ cup butter or margarine, melted
1 (6-ounce) package semi-sweet chocolate chips

In top of double boiler, melt the caramels in $^1/_3$ cup of the milk. Stir to blend; set aside. Combine dry cake mix, walnuts, melted butter and remaining $^1/_3$ cup milk. Divide and place half the mixture in bottom of greased 9x13-inch baking pan. Bake at 350° for 6 minutes. Remove from oven. Sprinkle chocolate chips over top. Spoon caramel mixture over chips.

This next step is a little tricky, but it does work. Take small amounts of the remaining cake mixture and press flat in the palm of your hand. Place over caramel mixture covering as much of the surface as you can. This layer will be thin, but it will cover—the end result is worth the effort. Bake at 350° for 15 to 20 minutes or until tests done. Do not overcook. Cool. Cut into squares.

CHOCOLATE BON BONS

FREEZE
TOP OF STOVE
CHILL

$^1/_4$ cup butter, softened
1 cup peanut butter
2 cups sifted powdered sugar
1 cup finely chopped peanuts
1 (12-ounce) package semi-sweet chocolate chips
1 tablespoon melted paraffin

Cream butter, peanut butter and powdered sugar. Stir in peanuts. If mixture is too soft, add a little more powdered sugar. Roll into small balls and place on cookie sheet. Put wooden toothpick in center of each ball and place in freezer. (This will make the dipping process much easier.) In top of double boiler, melt chocolate chips and paraffin and blend thoroughly. Remove 5 to 6 Bon Bons at a time from freezer. Dip one at a time in hot chocolate; remove excess by tapping edge of pan with side of toothpick. Place on waxed paper. Remove toothpick and fill in hole with additional chocolate, swirling to make a design. Place in refrigerator to set. Store in covered container in refrigerator or freeze. Makes about 7 dozen.
TIP: This is an easy recipe but time consuming. Make the Bon Bons one day and freeze. Then at your convenience dip in chocolate. Let the kids help, they'll love it.

BROWNIES   OVEN

> 1 cup butter or margarine, softened
> 2 cups sugar
> 3 (1-ounce) squares unsweetened chocolate, melted
> 4 eggs
> 1¹/₂ cups flour

Cream butter and sugar thoroughly. Add melted chocolate, then eggs. Stir in flour. Pour into greased 9x13-inch pan and bake at 350° for 25 minutes or until done. Do not overbake. Cool and cut into squares. Makes about 5 dozen.
VARIATION: Add 1 cup chopped walnuts.

CHOCOLATE WALNUT BROWNIES   TOP OF STOVE
                                                  OVEN

> 1 cup butter or margarine
> 1²/₃ cups semi-sweet chocolate chips, divided
> 2 cups sugar
> 3 eggs
> 1 cup flour
> 1 cup coarsely chopped walnuts

Melt butter and ²/₃ cup of the chocolate chips over very low heat. Remove from heat. Stir in sugar. Add eggs; stir until well mixed. Stir in flour and nuts. Pour into buttered 9x13-inch baking pan. Sprinkle with remaining 1 cup chocolate chips. Bake at 350° for 30 to 35 minutes or until tests done (do not overbake). Cool.

PEANUT BUTTER BARS   TOP OF STOVE
                                                  CHILL

> ¹/₂ cup light corn syrup
> ¹/₃ cup sugar
> ³/₄ cup peanut butter
> 1 teaspoon vanilla extract
> 1 cup Rice Krispies
> 2 cups Corn Flakes

Combine corn syrup and sugar in small saucepan. Cook until hot and sugar has melted. Stir in peanut butter and vanilla; mix until blended. Add remaining ingredients. Spread in buttered 8-inch square pan; chill until set. Cut in squares. Best stored in refrigerator. Makes about 3 dozen.
TIP: These are so good you'll probably want to double the recipe and use a 9x13-inch pan.

CHINESE COOKIES

TOP OF STOVE
CHILL

1 (6-ounce) package butterscotch chips
1 (6-ounce) package semi-sweet chocolate chips
1 cup chopped walnuts
1 (5-ounce) can Chow Mein Noodles

Melt chips in top of double boiler; stir until blended and smooth. Remove from heat. Add walnuts and Chow Mein Noodles; gently stir until evenly coated. Drop by teaspoon onto waxed paper-lined cookie sheet. Chill until firm. Makes about 5 dozen.
TIP: These must be stored in the refrigerator.

MOM'S PEANUT BUTTER COOKIES

OVEN

This is an unusual cookie because it doesn't have flour in the recipe.

1 cup peanut butter, smooth or crunchy
1 cup sugar
1 egg
1 teaspoon vanilla extract
$^1/_4$ cup semi-sweet chocolate chips
$^1/_4$ cup chopped walnuts

Combine ingredients and mix well. Drop by teaspoon onto ungreased baking sheet. Bake at 350° for 6 to 8 minutes or until batter starts to firm up and lightly brown. Makes about 2 $^1/_2$ dozen.

ALMOND BUTTER COOKIES

OVEN

A wonderful cookie you will want to make often.

1 ($18^1/_2$-ounce) box yellow cake mix
$^1/_2$ cup melted butter or margarine
$^1/_2$ cup chopped almonds
1 (16-ounce) box powdered sugar, sifted
1 (8-ounce) package cream cheese, softened
3 eggs, divided

In mixer bowl, blend cake mix, melted butter, almonds, and one of the eggs. Pat mixture into buttered 9x13-inch baking dish. Beat powdered sugar, cream cheese and remaining 2 eggs until well mixed; about 1 minute. Pour into baking dish, spreading evenly. Bake at 350° for 40 to 45 minutes or until lightly browned. Cool. Cut into squares.

CHOCOLATE COCONUT BARS

OVEN
TOP OF STOVE
CHILL

1½ cups graham cracker crumbs
½ cup butter or margarine, melted
2⅔ cups Angel Flake coconut
1 (14-ounce) can Eagle Brand sweetened condensed milk
1 (12-ounce) package semi-sweet chocolate chips
½ cup creamy peanut butter

Combine graham cracker crumbs and melted butter. Press into ungreased 9x13-inch baking dish. Sprinkle coconut over top. Pour condensed milk over coconut. Bake at 350° for 25 to 30 minutes or until lightly browned. Meanwhile, over low heat, melt the chocolate chips with the peanut butter. Pour over hot coconut layer. Chill until set. Cut into bars. Makes about 45 cookies.

CHOCOLATE PEANUT SQUARES

TOP OF STOVE
CHILL

Delicious! Reese's Peanut Butter Cups has competition.

¼ cup butter or margarine, melted
5½ double graham crackers, crushed fine
2 cups sifted powdered sugar
½ cup chunky peanut butter
1 (6-ounce) package semi-sweet chocolate chips

Pour melted butter over graham cracker crumbs, stirring to blend. Add powdered sugar and peanut butter; mix well. Pour into buttered 8-inch square pan, spreading evenly. Melt chocolate chips in top of double boiler. Spread over top of mixture. Chill until firm, but not hard, about 30 minutes. Cut into squares. Cover and chill until ready to serve. Makes 25 squares.

SHORTBREAD

OVEN

1 cup butter, softened
½ cup sifted powdered sugar
¼ teaspoon salt
¼ teaspoon baking powder
2 cups flour

In mixer bowl, cream butter and powdered sugar. Beat until light. Combine remaining ingredients; add to butter mixture. Beat until thoroughly blended. Divide mixture and pat evenly into two 9-inch pie pans. Prick all over with a fork. Bake at 350° for 15 to 20 minutes or until a very light golden color. Cut into pie shaped wedges. Serve hot or cold.

CUT-OUT COOKIES

 2 cups butter, softened (do not substitute)
 2 cups sugar
 4 eggs
 2 teaspoons vanilla extract
 1 teaspoon salt
 6 cups flour

In mixer bowl, cream butter until smooth. Gradually add sugar, mixing well after each addition. Beat until light and fluffy. Add eggs and vanilla and mix well. Combine salt and flour. Add to creamed mixture, a little at a time and mix well. Cover and chill at least 6 hours. On lightly floured surface, using a small amount of dough at a time, roll out to $1/8$-inch thickness. Cut out shapes with cookie cutters. Place on ungreased cookie sheets and bake at 375° for 8 to 10 minutes or until just beginning to brown around edges. Makes about 6 dozen cookies depending on size of cookie cutters.

TIP: If desired, cookies can be frosted or decorated.

LADYFINGERS

One of my favorite desserts, Ice Cream Cake, calls for ladyfingers which are impossible to find in the Washington area. This recipe is a very good substitute and quite easy to make.

 3 eggs, separated
 $1/4$ cup sugar, plus 2 tablespoons
 $1/2$ cup powdered sugar
 1 teaspoon vanilla extract
 $1/8$ teaspoon salt
 $3/4$ cup sifted flour

Beat egg yolks, the $1/4$ cup sugar, and the powdered sugar until a light yellow. Beat egg whites, vanilla, salt and remaining 2 tablespoons sugar until stiff but not dry. Fold egg yolk mixture into the egg whites. Gently fold in flour. Using a pastry bag fitted with a $1/2$-inch round tip, pipe $2 1/2$ to 3-inch strips of batter onto greased and floured baking sheets. Bake at 350° for 6 to 8 minutes or until just beginning to brown on the bottom. Let cool on baking sheets one minute, then remove and cool on rack. Makes $2 1/2$ to 3 dozen.

TIP: These are best when used same day made.

FINNISH JELLY FINGERS

CHILL
OVEN

I made hundreds of these for my daughter's wedding. They make a colorful addition to a cookie tray.

> 1 cup butter, softened
> 3/4 cup sugar
> 1 egg
> 2 1/2 cups flour
> 1 teaspoon baking powder
> Jam

In mixer bowl, cream butter and sugar. Add egg; beat thoroughly. Combine flour and baking powder. Add to butter mixture, stirring by hand. Cover and chill dough several hours or overnight. Divide dough into 5 or 6 parts. Knead dough slightly to make it more workable. Roll into long 1/2-inch thick rolls. Carefully place on cookie sheet, allowing about 4 inches between rolls. With the side of your finger, make a well lengthwise down the roll, pressing almost to the bottom. Fill well with jam. Bake at 375° for 10 to 12 minutes or until done but not brown. Remove from oven and carefully place each roll on a bread board. With a sharp knife cut diagonally into 1 1/4-inch strips. Cool on rack.
TIP: The color of jam can be your choice; red, green, yellow, etc. Cookies can be frozen. If you wish to drizzle the cookies with a powdered sugar glaze, freeze cookies but frost when ready to serve.

CANDIED WALNUTS

TOP OF STOVE

Do try these, they are delicious. Bet you can't eat just one!

> 1/2 cup sugar
> 1 cup firmly packed light brown sugar
> 1/2 cup sour cream
> 1 teaspoon vanilla extract
> 3 cups walnut halves

Combine sugar, brown sugar and sour cream in heavy medium size saucepan; stir to blend. Cook over medium heat, stirring constantly, until sugar is dissolved. Continue cooking, without stirring, to 238° on candy thermometer. Remove from heat; quickly stir in vanilla. Add walnuts and stir to coat. Turn out on waxed paper-lined baking sheet. Working with 2 forks, quickly separate walnuts. Let stand until set and coating is dry. Makes about 1 pound.
TIP: If walnuts halves are large, break in half.

CREAM CHEESE MINTS

1 (8-ounce) package cream cheese, softened
$^1/_2$-1 teaspoon desired flavoring
Food coloring
2 (1 pound) boxes powdered sugar, sifted
Granulated sugar

In mixing bowl, beat cream cheese until soft. Add desired flavoring and coloring. Gradually add powdered sugar, mixing until dough is very thick and heavy, but not dry. Roll in small balls; dip in granulated sugar. Press into small rubber molds; unmold. Experiment to get the size ball needed to fill mold. If mixture tends to stick, add more powdered sugar. Mints should unmold easily without sticking. Place mints on plate and allow to dry somewhat before storing in covered container in refrigerator or freezer. Makes about 130 mints.
TIP: Use yellow coloring with lemon flavoring, pink with peppermint, and green with mint. Molds can be found in speciality kitchen shops and baker's supply houses or catalogs. These are wonderful mints for weddings, showers, luncheons, hostess gifts, etc.

CHOCOLATE CARAMEL TURTLES

1 (16-ounce) package vanilla caramels
2 tablespoons water
$^3/_4$ pound pecan halves
1 (6-ounce) package semi-sweet chocolate chips

Melt caramels and water in top of double boiler, stirring occasionally until melted. Grease cookie sheet. Arrange 36 groups of pecan halves, about 2 inches apart, on cookie sheet. Drop melted caramel by teaspoon on top of nuts. Let cool. Melt chocolate chips in top of double boiler. Frost top of each turtle with melted chocolate. Cool. Makes 3 dozen.

BRIAN'S PEANUT BUTTER CANDY

Brian enjoyed making candy almost as much as he enjoyed making cookies.

1 cup peanut butter, smooth or crunchy
1 cup light corn syrup
1 cup powdered milk
1 cup (or more) sifted powdered sugar

Combine all ingredients and mix until thoroughly blended. Shape into balls and roll in extra powdered sugar. Place on baking sheet and chill until set. Makes about 3 dozen.

PEANUT BRITTLE

TOP OF STOVE

> 3 cups sugar
> 1 cup light corn syrup
> $^{1}/_{2}$ cup water
> 3 cups salted Spanish peanuts
> 2 teaspoons baking soda

Combine sugar, corn syrup and water in large heavy saucepan. Cook over medium heat to 280° or hardcrack stage. Gradually stir in peanuts and continue cooking to 300°. Turn off heat and gently, but quickly, stir in baking soda. Immediately pour onto 2 large greased cookie sheets. Do not spread, mixture will spread without any help. Let cool. Break into desired size pieces. Makes about 2 $^{1}/_{2}$ pounds.

MICROWAVE PEANUT BRITTLE

MICROWAVE

> 1 cup sugar
> $^{1}/_{2}$ cup light corn syrup
> 1$^{3}/_{4}$ cups Spanish peanuts
> 1 teaspoon butter
> 1 teaspoon vanilla extract
> 1 teaspoon baking soda

In 4 cup glass measuring cup, combine sugar and corn syrup. Cook on high 4 minutes. Add peanuts and cook 4 minutes. Add butter and vanilla; cook 1 minute. Quickly fold in baking soda. Spread on greased cookie sheet to cool. Break into pieces.
VARIATION: Use cashews or dry roasted peanuts.

SNOWBALLS

TOP OF STOVE
CHILL

> 1 (6-ounce) package semi-sweet chocolate chips
> $^{1}/_{3}$ cup canned evaporated milk
> 1 cup sifted powdered sugar
> $^{1}/_{2}$ cup finely chopped walnuts
> 1$^{1}/_{4}$ cups Angel Flake coconut

Combine chocolate chips and milk in top of double boiler. Heat until melted, stirring to blend. Remove from heat. Stir in powdered sugar and walnuts. Cool slightly (until mixture begins to hold its shape). Drop by teaspoon onto mound of coconut. Roll in coconut; form into balls. Chill until set. Makes 2$^{1}/_{2}$ to 3 dozen.

EASY FUDGE

5^1/$_2$ cups sifted powdered sugar
^{1}/$_2$ cup butter, melted
2 eggs, slightly beaten
1^1/$_2$ cups semi-sweet chocolate chips, melted
1 teaspoon vanilla extract
1 cup chopped walnuts

Combine powdered sugar, butter and eggs; mix thoroughly. Stir in melted chocolate. Add vanilla and walnuts. Pour into buttered 9-inch square pan. Let stand until set. Cut into small squares. Makes about 3 ^{1}/$_2$ dozen pieces.

CREAMY FUDGE   CHILL

2 (3-ounce) packages cream cheese, softened
2 tablespoons milk
4 cups sifted powdered sugar
4 (1-ounce) squares unsweetened chocolate, melted
1 teaspoon vanilla extract
2 cups coarsely chopped walnuts

Combine cream cheese and powdered sugar in mixer bowl; mix until thoroughly blended. Add melted chocolate and vanilla. Stir in walnuts. Spread in foil-lined and buttered 8-inch square pan. Chill several hours or overnight. Remove from pan and cut into small squares. Makes about 3 ^{1}/$_2$ dozen pieces.

EASY TOFFEE   TOP OF STOVE

2 cups finely chopped walnuts, divided
1 cup firmly packed light brown sugar
^{3}/$_4$ cup butter
1^1/$_4$ cups semi-sweet or milk chocolate chips

Sprinkle 1 cup of the walnuts evenly in well buttered 9-inch square dish. Combine brown sugar and butter in small heavy saucepan. Bring to a boil over medium heat. Cook, stirring occasionally, to hard-ball stage, about 266° on a candy thermometer. Pour hot mixture evenly over walnuts. Sprinkle chocolate chips over top. Sprinkle remaining 1 cup walnuts over the chocolate chips. Press mixture down firmly using a knife or metal spatula. Let stand until firm (or chill). Break into small pieces.
TIP: This doesn't last that long around our house, but will keep several weeks in a covered container.

DIVINITY

2 cups sugar
$1/2$ cup light corn syrup
$1/2$ cup water
1 egg white, stiffly beaten
1 teaspoon vanilla extract
1 cup chopped walnuts or pecans

In heavy saucepan, combine sugar, corn syrup and water. Bring to a boil and cook to 240° on candy thermometer. Pour mixture over stiffly beaten egg white. Beat with mixer until it starts to lose it gloss. Add vanilla and nuts. Drop by teaspoon onto buttered cookie sheet.
TIP: Best if not made on a rainy day.

EASY POPCORN BALLS

$1/4$ cup butter or margarine
$1/2$ teaspoon vanilla extract
1 ($10^1/_2$-ounce) package marshmallows
6 quarts popped popcorn (approx.)

Combine butter, vanilla, and marshmallows in top of double boiler. Stir until melted and smooth. Pour over popcorn. Butter hands and form into balls, but be careful mixture may be hot. Makes 12 to 15 balls.

CARAMEL CORN

2 cups firmly packed light brown sugar
1 cup butter
1 teaspoon salt
$1/2$ cup light corn syrup
1 teaspoon baking soda
6 quarts popped popcorn

Combine first 4 ingredients in heavy saucepan. Bring to a boil and cook 5 minutes, stirring occasionally. Remove from heat and stir in baking soda. Pour over popcorn; stir until coated. Spread on large cookie sheet or in roasting pan. Bake at 200° for 60 minutes, stirring every 15 minutes. Remove from oven and let cool. Makes 6 quarts.
TIP: This may seem like a lot of caramel corn, but it really isn't. It goes very fast. If desired, add peanuts, pecans, walnuts, cashews or a mixture of nuts to popcorn before mixing with syrup mixture.

Brunch & Lunch

BASIC OMELET

3 eggs
$^1/_2$ teaspoon salt
$^1/_8$ teaspoon pepper
1 teaspoon water
1 tablespoon butter

Slowly heat a 8 or 9-inch curved-sided non-stick skillet over medium heat. The pan must be hot enough for the butter to sizzle but not brown. Combine first 4 ingredients in small bowl, mixing with fork until whites and yolks are just blended. Add butter to skillet; increase heat slightly. When melted, add eggs all at once. As eggs begin to set, pull edges slightly up and toward the center, letting uncooked egg flow underneath. When eggs are lightly set, fold in half and serve. Makes 1 omelet. TIP: Any filling such as cheese, ham, onion, green pepper, mushrooms, etc. can be added to top of omelet just before the eggs start to set.

FRITTATA

6 eggs
1 cup milk
1 tablespoon butter, melted
$^1/_4$ teaspoon salt
$^1/_8$ teaspoon pepper
1 cup (4-ounces) grated Cheddar cheese

With wire whisk, beat first 5 ingredients until blended. Pour into a greased deep dish 10-inch pie plate. Sprinkle cheese over top. Bake at 400° for 20 minutes or until set and lightly browned. Makes 4 servings. TIP: For variety, sprinkle top with parsley, ham, bacon, or sausage and cheese. Sliced vegetables and mushrooms can also be added.

COMPANY SWISS EGGS

2 cups (8-ounces) grated Gruyére or Swiss cheese
$^1/_4$ cup butter
1 cup whipping cream
$^1/_2$ teaspoon salt
$^1/_8$ teaspoon pepper
12 eggs, slightly beaten

Sprinkle cheese evenly in buttered 9x13-inch baking dish. Dot with butter. Combine cream, salt and pepper. Pour half of cream over cheese. Pour eggs over top; pour in remaining cream. Bake at 325° for 30 to 35 minutes or until eggs are set. Makes 8 to 10 servings.

HEAT AND HOLD SCRAMBLED EGGS   TOP OF STOVE

$^1/_4$ cup butter (do not substitute)
12 eggs
$1^1/_3$ cups milk
1 teaspoon salt
$^1/_8$ teaspoon pepper
2 tablespoons flour

Melt butter in large skillet over low heat. Combine remaining ingredients in mixing bowl; mix until smooth. Pour mixture into skillet. As eggs cook, lift outside edges to allow uncooked eggs to flow to outer edge of skillet. Continue stirring until eggs are cooked, but mixture still has a creamy appearance. Serve, or cover and keep warm until serving time. Makes 6 servings.
TIP: For variety, press ground pork sausage firmly into a ring mold; bake at 350° for 45 to 60 minutes or until thoroughly cooked. Drain off fat. Unmold on serving plate and fill center with the scrambled eggs.

SCRAMBLED EGGS   TOP OF STOVE

8 eggs
$^3/_4$ teaspoon salt
$^1/_8$ teaspoon pepper
$^1/_2$ cup milk
2 tablespoons butter or margarine

Combine first 4 ingredients. Beat with fork just till yolks and whites are blended. Melt butter in large skillet. Add eggs and cook over low heat. Stir gently with spoon, cooking just until eggs are set and still moist. Serve immediately. Makes 4 servings.

EGG NESTS   OVEN

12 slices bread
12 eggs
Salt and pepper
6 teaspoons butter or margarine

Grease a 12-cup muffin tin. Remove crust from bread. Place one bread slice in each muffin cup; push down gently so it looks like a cup with four corners. Drop a raw egg into each cup. Sprinkle with salt and pepper. Top each egg with $^1/_2$ teaspoon butter. Bake at 350° for 15 minutes or until eggs are cooked and bread is toasted. Makes 6 servings.
TIP: Recipe can be easily adjusted for a smaller number of servings. If you have the larger size muffin cups, use those. If not, use small size eggs, to prevent the egg white from running over onto the tins.

SAUSAGE GRAVY   TOP OF STOVE

>   1 pound bulk pork sausage
>   2 cups milk
>   4 tablespoons flour
> $^1/_2$ teaspoon salt
> $^1/_4$ teaspoon pepper
>   Hot biscuits

In large skillet, crumble sausage into small pieces and brown. Remove sausage and drain off all but 4 tablespoons of the drippings. To the drippings in skillet, stir in the flour. Keep stirring until mixture is smooth and simmers. Add milk, a little at a time, stirring quickly to make a smooth gravy. Add salt and pepper. Cook, stirring constantly, until mixture is desired thickness for gravy. Add sausage. Split hot biscuits; place on serving plate. Pour gravy over top. Makes 4 servings.

MAKE YOUR OWN SAUSAGE   CHILL
                                                TOP OF STOVE

A mildly seasoned sausage. Make day ahead so flavors will have a chance to blend.

>   2 pounds freshly ground pork
> $^3/_4$ teaspoon salt
> $^3/_4$ teaspoon freshly ground black pepper
> $^1/_4$ teaspoon red pepper (cayenne)
>   1 teaspoon dried leaf thyme
>   1 teaspoon dried sage

Combine ingredients and mix thoroughly. Chill overnight. Make into patties and cook over medium heat until lightly browned.
TIP: Patties can be frozen. Delicious on home made pizza.

SAUSAGE BRUNCH SOUFFLE   TOP OF STOVE
                                                CHILL
> $1^1/_2$ pounds seasoned bulk pork sausage   OVEN
>   6 slices white bread with crust, cubed
>   6 eggs
>   2 cups milk
>   1 tablespoon dry mustard
>   1 cup (4-ounces) grated Cheddar cheese

Brown sausage and drain off fat. Place bread cubes in greased 12x8-inch baking dish. Slightly beat eggs. Add remaining ingredients along with the sausage. Pour over bread cubes. Evenly distribute the mixture, pushing down to coat all the ingredients. Cover and chill several hours or overnight. When ready to serve, bake at 350° for 40 to 45 minutes or until lightly browned and mixture is set. Makes 6 servings.

CINNAMON SUGAR OATMEAL   TOP OF STOVE

> **2 cups quick oats (1 minute type)**
> **2 tablespoons sugar**
> **$1/2$ teaspoon cinnamon**
> **$2/3$ cup half and half**
> **Butter**
> **Light brown sugar**

In medium saucepan, bring 2 $1/2$ cups water to a boil. Stirring constantly, gradually add the dry oatmeal. Add sugar and cinnamon; mix well. Cook 1 minute. Add half and half and reheat to boiling. Pour into individual serving dishes. Top each with a dab of butter and a sprinkle of brown sugar. Makes 6 servings unless you are really hungry, then it makes 4 servings.

BACON PIZZA QUICHE   OVEN

A great pizza for breakfast, lunch or dinner.

> **Single pastry for 9-inch pie crust**
> **12 slices bacon, cooked and crumbled**
> **2 cups (8-ounces) grated Swiss cheese**
> **$1^1/3$ cups sour cream**
> **4 eggs**
> **1 teaspoon dried parsley**

Roll out pastry to a 13-inch circle. Place in 12 inch pizza pan. Press edges against side. Turn over excess dough, forming a thicker crust on inside edge of pan. Bake at 425° for 5 minutes. Cool. Sprinkle bacon over crust, then the cheese. Combine remaining ingredients; mix well. Pour over cheese. Bake at 425°, on lowest rack of oven, for 20 to 25 minutes or until set. Makes 4 to 6 servings.

NO-CRUST SPINACH QUICHE   OVEN

> **2 cups whipping cream**
> **6 eggs**
> **$1/2$ cup fresh white bread crumbs**
> **$1/2$ teaspoon salt**
> **2 tablespoons frozen orange juice concentrate**
> **1 cup finely torn fresh spinach leaves**

In large mixing bowl, beat cream and eggs. Add remaining ingredients and pour into buttered quiche dish or 10-inch, deep pie dish. Bake at 350° for 35 to 40 minutes or until custard is set and lightly browned. Makes 6 servings.

QUICHE LORRAINE
OVEN

My favorite Quiche. Serve with fresh fruit or a spinach salad and toasted French bread.

1 deep dish 9-inch pie shell
1^1/$_2$ cups (6-ounces) grated Swiss cheese
12 slices cooked bacon, crumbled
4 eggs, beaten slightly
1^1/$_4$ cups whipping cream
^{1}/$_2$ cup milk

Sprinkle grated cheese evenly over pastry shell. Sprinkle bacon over top. Combine eggs, cream and milk, stirring to blend thoroughly. Pour mixture over bacon. Bake at 325° for 40 minutes or until filling appears firm when pan is gently shaken. Makes 6 servings.
TIP: To prevent a soggy crust, you may prefer to prebake pie crust. Prick crust with fork and bake at 400° for 10 minutes. Cool.

SWEDISH PANCAKES
CHILL
TOP OF STOVE

2 cups flour
4 eggs
^{1}/$_4$ cup sugar
^{1}/$_2$ teaspoon salt
2 cups milk
^{1}/$_4$ cup melted butter, plus additional butter for frying

In large mixer bowl, combine flour, eggs, sugar, salt and 1^1/$_2$ cups of the milk. Mix at medium speed until blended. Add remaining ^{1}/$_2$ cup milk and the ^{1}/$_4$ cup butter. Cover and chill several hours or overnight. Batter should be fairly thin. If necessary, add a little more milk. Preheat skillet; add small dab of butter and spread to cover bottom. Pour about ^{1}/$_4$ cup batter into skillet; spread thin by tipping pan, working quickly. When pancake appears a little dry on top, turn and cook other side. Roll up and keep warm while preparing remaining pancakes. Serve with butter and syrup. Makes about 12 large pancakes.

FRENCH TOAST
TOP OF STOVE

2 eggs
^{1}/$_2$ cup whipping cream
^{1}/$_8$ teaspoon salt
6 slices French bread, cut ^{3}/$_4$ to 1-inch thick
Butter

Combine first 3 ingredients. Dip bread in egg mixture, coating well on both sides. Cook in generous amount of butter, about ^{1}/$_8$-inch deep, until golden brown on each side. Makes 2 to 3 servings.

OVEN PANCAKES   OVEN

If you haven't had these pancakes before, you are in for a treat. Makes a great breakfast or light dinner. Serve with fruit or bacon and sausage links.

> **For each Pancake:**
> $1/2$ **cup flour**
> $1/2$ **cup milk**
> **2 eggs**
> **Dash salt**
> $1/4$ **cup butter**

Combine flour and milk in small mixing bowl; mix with fork just until blended (batter will still be lumpy). Stir in eggs and salt. Place butter in 9-inch pie pan and melt in 425° oven. Remove from oven; pour in batter. Bake 15 minutes or until puffed and golden. Serve immediately. Pancake will puff up, but will fall shortly after taking from oven. Makes 1 to 2 servings.
TIP: Sprinkle with lemon juice and powdered sugar; serve with maple syrup or fruit.

PANCAKE MIX

> $7^{1}/2$ **cups all-purpose flour**
> $1/4$ **cup baking powder**
> **1 tablespoon plus 1 teaspoon salt**
> $2/3$ **cup sugar**

Combine ingredients in large bowl. Stir to mix thoroughly. Store mix in an airtight container at cool room temperature. Makes about $8^{1}/2$ cups mix.

PANCAKES (FROM "PANCAKE MIX")   TOP OF STOVE

> **1 egg, beaten slightly**
> **1 cup milk**
> **2 tablespoons butter, melted**
> $1^{1}/4$ **cups Pancake Mix**

Combine egg and milk; stir to blend. Add melted butter. Stir in Pancake Mix with fork, just until dry ingredients are moistened. Batter should be slightly lumpy. If batter seems a little thin, add more mix. For medium-large pancakes, use $1/4$ to $1/3$ cup batter for each pancake and bake on lightly oiled griddle or skillet, turning once, until golden brown. Makes 6 to 7 pancakes.
TIP: Double or triple recipe as needed.

PASTA CARBONARA   TOP OF STOVE

For a smooth creamy sauce, butter, cream and Parmesan must stand at room temperature for 2 hours.

8 ounces thin fettuccine noodles
2 eggs
2 tablespoons whipping cream
2 tablespoons butter
5 slices bacon, cooked and crumbled
$^1/_2$ cup freshly grated Parmesan cheese

Cook fettucine according to package directions. Meanwhile, combine eggs and cream. Drain pasta and put in large heated serving bowl. Toss with the butter. Add egg mixture and toss quickly to coat. Quickly stir in bacon and Parmesan. Serve immediately. Makes 6 side dish servings or 3 to 4 main dish servings.

CHICKEN FETTUCCINE   TOP OF STOVE

1 (12-ounce) package thin fettuccine noodles
$^1/_2$ cup butter
$^1/_2$ cup grated Mozzarella cheese
$^1/_2$ cup whipping cream
2 cups cooked cubed chicken
$^1/_3$ cup freshly grated Parmesan cheese

Cook fettuccine as directed on package. Meanwhile, in small heavy saucepan, melt butter. Add Mozzarella cheese and cream. Cook over low heat until smooth and mixture thickens slightly. Drain noodles. Place in a large bowl. Add sauce and chicken. Place noodles on serving dishes and sprinkle with Parmesan cheese. Serve immediately. Makes 4 servings.

BAKED FETTUCCINE   TOP OF STOVE
                                                      OVEN

8 ounces fettucini noodles
$^1/_4$ cup butter or margarine, softened
$^1/_2$ cup milk
2 eggs, beaten
6 tablespoons grated Parmesan cheese, divided
1 tablespoon seasoned bread crumbs

Cook noodles according to package directions; drain and return to pan. Stir in butter. Add milk, eggs and 5 tablespoons Parmesan. Pour into greased 8x8-inch baking dish. Combine remaining Parmesan and bread crumbs. Sprinkle over noodles. Bake at 350° for 20 to 25 minutes or until set. Makes 4 to 6 servings.

RIGATONI BAKE

Serve with toasted French bread, tossed green salad and fruit compote and you have a complete meal in less than an hour.

> 8 ounces uncooked rigatoni macaroni, about $1^1/_4$-inches in length
> 8 ounce block Cheddar cheese
> 1 (15.5-ounce) jar spaghetti sauce
> 3 tablespoons grated Parmesan cheese

Cook rigatoni as directed on package. Drain and rinse thoroughly. Cut cheese into strips $1^1/_4$-inches long by $^1/_4$-inch thick. Insert a strip of cheese in each cooked rigatoni and place in greased $1^1/_2$-quart baking dish. Pour sauce over top and sprinkle with Parmesan cheese. Bake, uncovered, at 350° for 25 to 30 minutes or until heated through. Makes 6 to 8 servings.

TIP: If you must have meat with your meal, brown one pound lean ground beef and add to the sauce. Vary by substituting 1 cup (4-ounces) grated Mozzarella cheese for the Parmesan.

SPINACH TORTELLINI WITH TOMATO SAUCE

This dish will add a lot of color and flavor to your menu.

> 1 tablespoon olive oil
> 1 large clove garlic, minced
> 2 (14.5-ounce) cans whole Italian style tomatoes, cut up
> 1 tablespoon sugar
> 1 (8-ounce) package spinach tortellini with cheese

Heat olive oil in medium saucepan. Add minced garlic and cook a couple minutes, but do not brown. Add tomatoes (do not drain); stir in sugar. Bring to a boil; reduce heat and simmer about 45 minutes or until thickened. Meanwhile, cook tortellini according to package directions. Drain and rinse thoroughly. Place tortellini on large serving platter and top with some of the tomato sauce. Makes 4 servings.

TIP: Leftover sauce can be refrigerated or frozen.

BROCCOLI-CHEESE SOUP

TOP OF STOVE

$1^1/_2$ cups fresh broccoli, chopped
$1/_4$ cup finely chopped onion
$5^1/_2$ cups milk
2 tablespoons butter or margarine
1 tablespoon flour
2 cups (8-ounces) grated Swiss cheese

In large saucepan, cook broccoli and onion in the milk until vegetables are tender. In small saucepan, melt butter. Stir in flour and heat until mixture bubbles and is smooth. Add to milk mixture; mix well. Bring mixture to a boil, reduce heat, simmer 3 to 4 minutes, stirring frequently. Remove from heat. Gradually add the cheese, stirring to melt. Serve hot. Makes 6 servings.

CHINESE EGG SOUP

TOP OF STOVE

4 cups seasoned chicken broth
$1/_2$ cup frozen green peas
1 egg, beaten

Bring chicken broth and peas to a boil in large saucepan. Slowly add egg to the boiling broth, stirring constantly. Serve hot. Makes 6 servings. TIP: If desired, add sliced mushrooms.

CHICKEN VELVET SOUP

TOP OF STOVE

$1/_3$ cup butter
$3/_4$ cup flour
6 cups hot chicken broth
2 cups milk
2 cups small cubed cooked chicken
Salt and pepper

Melt butter in heavy Dutch Oven or large saucepan. Add flour; stir quickly to blend. Cook over low heat until smooth. Add 2 cups of the chicken stock; stir to keep mixture smooth. Add milk. Cook, stirring frequently, until thickened. Add remaining 4 cups chicken stock and the cubed chicken. Continue cooking until heated through. Add salt and pepper to taste. Makes 8 servings.
TIP: For a richer soup, use half milk and half cream. For added color, stir in 2 to 3 drops yellow food coloring.

CHEESE NUT SOUP

TOP OF STOVE

> 3 tablespoons butter
> 4 cups whipping cream
> 2 small garlic cloves, minced
> 4 cups (16-ounces) grated Cheddar cheese
> 4 egg yolks
> 1/4 cup finely chopped walnuts

Place butter in top of double boiler. Add 2 cups of the cream, garlic and cheese. Cook over hot water until cheese is melted. Combine remaining cream with egg yolks; add to cheese mixture, stirring constantly, until hot (do not allow soup to boil). Serve immediately topped with a sprinkle of walnuts. Makes 6 to 8 servings.

CLAM CHOWDER

TOP OF STOVE

> 1 1/2 quarts chicken broth
> 1 pint finely chopped clams
> 2 cups small diced potatoes
> 1/2 cup small diced carrots
> 4 cups half and half
> Salt and pepper

Combine first 4 ingredients in large saucepan. Cook until vegetables are tender and mixture has thickened. Stir in half and half. Add salt and pepper to taste. Makes 6 to 8 servings.

FRENCH ONION SOUP

TOP OF STOVE
BROIL

A whole meal when served with a salad and fresh fruit.

> 5 medium onions
> 3 tablespoons butter
> 4 cups rich beef broth
> Salt and pepper
> Toasted French bread slices or croutons
> 1 cup (4-ounces) grated Swiss or Mozzarella cheese

Thinly slice onions; separate into rings. Heat butter in 3-quart pot and cook onions until tender and light golden. Add broth. Season with salt and pepper. Bring to a boil, reduce heat and simmer 10 minutes. Top with bread slices; sprinkle with cheese. Place under broiler and cook until cheese is melted and lightly browned. Makes 4 servings.
TIP: You can also put soup in individual oven-proof dishes and top with bread and cheese.

CREAMY POTATO SOUP

8 slices bacon
1 cup finely chopped onion
4 cups cubed potatoes
2 cans cream of chicken soup
2 soup cans milk
Salt and pepper

In 3-quart saucepan, cook bacon until crisp; remove bacon and set aside. Pour off all but 3 tablespoons fat; add onions and brown. Add potatoes and about 1 1/2 cups water or enough to cover. Cook, covered, until potatoes are tender, 15 to 20 minutes. Combine soup and milk; stir until smooth. Add to potato mixture. Heat but do not boil. Add salt and pepper to taste. Crumble bacon; stir in just before serving soup or sprinkle on top to garnish. Makes 6 servings.

GROUND BEEF SOUP

1¹/₂ pounds lean ground beef
1 medium onion, chopped
2 cups cubed potatoes
1 ¹/₂ cups sliced carrots
1 (1 pound 12-ounce) can tomatoes, cut up
Salt and pepper

Brown ground beef and onion; drain off fat. Put meat mixture, potatoes, carrots and tomatoes in large pot. Stir in 2 to 3 cups of water. Cook 1 hour or until vegetables are tender. Add salt and pepper to taste. Makes 6 servings.
TIP: To expand recipe you can add thinly sliced celery and any leftover vegetables such as peas and corn. Serve with French bread.

ORIENTAL BEEF NOODLE SOUP

A filling soup to make on those days when you have 30 minutes or less to prepare dinner.

1 pound lean ground beef
1 (3-ounce) package oriental noodles with beef flavor
4 cups beef or chicken broth
1 (10-ounce) package frozen mixed vegetables
¹/₃ cup thinly sliced celery
2 tablespoons soy sauce

Brown ground beef; drain off fat. Meanwhile, in large saucepan, break up the noodles. Add the seasoning packet and remaining ingredients. Stir in 1 cup water. Bring to a boil. Add ground beef. Reduce heat; simmer 4 to 5 minutes or until vegetables are tender. Makes 6 servings.

TORTILLA TURNOVERS
TOP OF STOVE
OVEN
1 pound lean ground beef
1 (1¼-ounce) package Taco seasoning mix
6 flour tortillas
2 cups (8-ounces) Cheddar cheese, grated
6 tablespoons chopped onion
6 tablespoons Salsa (or more)

Brown ground beef, mashing meat slightly so that you have small pieces of meat rather than large. Drain off fat. Add seasoning mix and ³/₄ cup water. Bring to a simmer and cook until most of the liquid is absorbed, about 15 minutes. Place tortillas on ungreased baking sheets. In center of each, place a portion of the meat mixture. Sprinkle meat with cheese, onion and salsa. Bake at 500° just until cheese melts. This takes a minute or so; you don't want the tortillas to crisp. Remove from oven and fold each tortilla in half like a turnover. Press edges. The melted cheese will seal the turnover. Makes 6 servings.

VEGIE PITA SANDWICH

My daughter loves these, especially on a hot summer day.

For each sandwich:
1 Pita bread
Creamed cheese, softened
Thinly sliced cucumber
Alfalfa sprouts
Sliced Swiss cheese
Thinly sliced tomatoes

Spread inside of each Pita with a thin layer of cream cheese. Add remaining ingredients and enjoy.
TIP: Most refreshing if ingredients are chilled.

YUMMY HOT DOGS
1 package refrigerated Crescent rolls
4 teaspoons melted butter or margarine
4 teaspoons prepared mustard
8 wieners
Sesame seeds

Separate crescents into 8 rolls. Brush each with melted butter and spread with mustard. Place wiener on wide end and roll toward narrow end. Place on ungreased baking sheet. Brush with melted butter and sprinkle with sesame seeds. Bake at 375° for 12 to 14 minutes or until rolls are lightly browned. Makes 8.

BAKED HAM SANDWICHES

$^1/_4$ cup butter, softened
1$^1/_2$ teaspoons prepared mustard
$^1/_2$ teaspoon poppy seeds
4 hamburger buns
4 thin slices ham
4 thin slices Swiss cheese

Combine first 3 ingredients; spread on hamburger buns. Place slice of ham and slice of cheese on each bun. Wrap each separately in foil or place in baking pan and cover with foil. Bake at 350° for 20 minutes or until heated through. Makes 4 sandwiches.

CHICKEN PINEAPPLE SANDWICHES

2 cups finely diced cooked chicken
1 (8-ounce) can crushed pineapple, drained
$^1/_4$ cup chopped slivered almonds
Mayonnaise
Alfalfa sprouts
Choice of bread, buttered

Combine first 3 ingredients in small bowl. Add just enough mayonnaise to moisten. Spread on half the bread slices; top with sprouts. Place remaining bread slices on top. Cut sandwiches in half diagonally. Makes 4 to 6 sandwiches.
TIP: Serve with relish tray, chips and a pitcher of ice cold tea.

BANANA-MUFFIN TREAT

Yummy!

4 English muffins
Butter or margarine
2 bananas, sliced
8 slices Swiss cheese
8 slices bacon, cooked, cut in half

Toast and lightly butter muffins. Place on baking sheet. Distribute banana slices evenly on muffins. Top each muffin with a slice of cheese. Criss-cross 2 slices bacon on each. Place under broiler just long enough to melt the cheese. Makes 2 to 4 servings.

FRENCH TOASTED SANDWICHES   TOP OF STOVE

4 thin slices ham (to fit bread)
4 thin slices cheese (to fit bread)
8 slices buttered bread
2 eggs, slightly beaten
$^1/_2$ cup milk or cream
Butter

Place slice of ham and cheese between 2 slices bread making 4 sandwiches. Combine eggs and milk. Dip sandwiches in egg mixture. Brown on both sides in heavy skillet or on grill, using butter as needed. Makes 4 sandwiches.

GOURMET CHICKEN SANDWICHES

16 thin slices cooked chicken or turkey breasts
1 (20-ounces) can pineapple spears, drained, reserve 1 tablespoon syrup
8 slices raisin bread, buttered
$^1/_3$ cup mayonnaise
2 tablespoons finely chopped pecans

Arrange chicken slices on each of 4 slices of bread. Top with well drained pineapple spears. Combine mayonnaise, the 1 tablespoon pineapple syrup, and pecans. Spread mixture evenly over remaining 4 slices of bread. Cut sandwiches in half and serve. Makes 4 sandwiches.

MEXICAN MUFFINS   TOP OF STOVE
                                       OVEN

1 pound lean ground beef
1 ($1^1/_4$-ounce) package Taco seasoning mix
$^1/_2$ cup water
5 English muffins, split
1 cup (4-ounces) grated Cheddar cheese

Brown ground beef; drain. Add seasoning mix and water. Simmer 15 minutes or until liquid is absorbed. Place muffins on cookie sheet; top with meat mixture. Sprinkle cheese over top. Bake at 350° for 10 minutes or until heated through. Makes 5 servings.
TIP: For a Mexican Hamburger, substitute hamburger buns for the English muffins; do not bake.

POLISH SAUSAGE SANDWICHES

1 tablespoon olive oil
$^3/_4$ cup chopped onion
$^1/_4$ cup chopped green pepper
$^1/_3$ cup drained Sauerkraut
2 cooked Polish sausages, heated
2 hot dog buns or hard rolls, split, warmed

Heat oil in small skillet. Sauté onion and green pepper until tender, but not brown. Stir in sauerkraut and heat through. Place sausages on buns and top with vegetable mixture. Makes 2 servings.

TUNA BURGERS

1 (6-ounce) can tuna, drained
$^1/_4$ cup finely chopped celery
$^1/_2$ cup (2-ounces) grated Cheddar cheese
$^1/_2$ small onion, finely chopped
$^1/_3$ cup mayonnaise (or to moisten)
6 hamburger buns

Combine first 5 ingredients and gently mix to blend. Fill buns with mixture. Wrap each separately in foil or place in baking pan and cover with foil. Bake at 350° for 20 minutes or until heated through. Makes 6 sandwiches.

SPOON BURGERS TOP OF STOVE

1 pound lean ground beef
1 can chicken gumbo soup
$^1/_4$ teaspoon salt
1 tablespoon prepared mustard
2 tablespoons catsup
6 hamburger buns

Brown ground beef in small skillet; drain off fat. Add remaining ingredients and simmer for 20 to 30 minutes, stirring occasionally. Serve on heated hamburger buns. Makes 6 servings.

TORTILLA PIZZA OVEN

Flour tortillas make a great crust for quick pizzas. You may be surprised at how good they are. Toppings are endless, just use your imagination and have fun.

Flour tortillas
Pizza sauce, canned or see Index
Mozzarella cheese, grated
Choice of meat
Choice of vegetable
Grated Parmesan cheese

Place tortillas on baking sheet and bake at 400° for 5 to 6 minutes or until lightly toasted. Remove from oven and turn over. Spread with pizza sauce. Sprinkle cheese over sauce. Top with meat and/or vegetables. Sprinkle with grated Parmesan. Increase heat to 450°. Bake pizzas 10 to 12 minutes or until cheese melts and pizza is lightly browned.

Meat choices:	Vegetable choices:
Cooked ground beef	Mushrooms
Cooked sausage	Onions
Canadian bacon	Red, yellow or green pepper
Pepperoni	Sliced tomatoes
Bacon	Ripe olives
Ham	Avocado

Meats & Seafoods

STUFFED GREEN PEPPERS

4 large green peppers
1$^1/_2$ pounds lean ground beef
1 cup chopped onion
$^1/_2$ cup cooked rice
Salt and pepper to taste
2 (8-ounce) cans tomato sauce

Cut green peppers in half lengthwise. Remove seeds. Cook in boiling water 5 minutes to slightly soften; drain. Meanwhile, brown ground beef and onion; drain off fat. Add cooked rice; season to taste. Place green peppers, cut side up, in 7x11-inch baking dish. Fill with meat mixture. Pour tomato sauce over top. Add $^1/_4$ cup water to baking dish. Bake at 325° for 60 minutes or until peppers are tender. Makes 4 servings.

MEXICAN SCRAMBLE

1 pound lean ground beef
1 medium onion, chopped
1 (16-ounce) can cream corn
1 (8-ounce) can tomato sauce
$^1/_2$ teaspoon chili powder
Salt and pepper

Brown ground beef and onion; drain. Stir in remaining ingredients and simmer about 15 minutes. Makes 4 servings.
TIP: Serve over mashed potatoes, noodles or rice.

EASY LASAGNE

An excellent lasagne recipe that doesn't take all day to make.

2 pounds lean ground beef
1 tablespoon light brown sugar
1 (32-ounce) jar spaghetti sauce with mushrooms
10-12 Lasagne noodles, cooked
2$^1/_2$ cups (10-ounces) grated Cheddar cheese
3 cups (12-ounces) grated Mozzarella cheese

Brown ground beef in large skillet; drain off fat. Stir in brown sugar and spaghetti sauce. Bring to a boil; reduce heat and simmer 20 minutes. Meanwhile, cook noodles according to directions on package. Spread about $^1/_2$ cup of the meat sauce in greased 9x13-inch deep baking dish. Layer starting with noodles, then sauce, Cheddar cheese and Mozzarella cheese, making 2 layers of everything. Bake at 375° for 30 minutes or until hot. Makes 10 to 12 servings.

HAMBURGER HOT DISH

1¹/₂ pounds lean ground beef
³/₄ cup finely chopped onion
1 cup sour cream
1 can cream of mushroom soup
1 can cream of chicken soup
4 cups noodles, cooked, drained

Brown ground beef and onion in large skillet; drain off fat. Stir in remaining ingredients. Pour into greased 3-quart casserole or 9x13-inch shallow baking dish. Bake at 350° for 45 minutes or until heated through. Makes 6 to 8 servings.
TIP: You can do all kinds of things with this casserole. Add any combination of chopped green pepper, pimiento, olives, corn, etc. Use regular or spiral shaped noodles. If desired, sprinkle top with buttered soft bread crumbs or grated cheese.

EASY GOULASH

Easy but good. Great for boating and camping.

1 pound lean ground beef
1 can kidney beans, drained
1 can vegetable soup

Brown ground beef in skillet; drain off fat. Add kidney beans and soup. Simmer 15 to 20 minutes. Makes 6 servings.

TACO CASSEROLE

1 (11-ounce) package corn chips, crushed
4 medium tomatoes, chopped
1 large onion, sliced
1 head lettuce, torn into bite-size pieces
3 (16-ounce) cans chili with beans
2 pounds sharp Cheddar cheese, grated

In two buttered 3-quart casseroles, arrange the ingredients in layers in order given, dividing evenly between the two casseroles. Bake at 425° for 25 minutes or until hot and cheese is melted. Makes 12 servings.
TIP: Have ingredients on hand for drop-in company. You can prepare this ahead of time to pop in the oven when ready.

EASY MEXICAN DISH ✓

The flavor combination of this one is really good — you'll want to make it often.

1 (12-ounce) can Mexican style corn, drained
2 (15-ounce) cans chili with beans
1 (8¹/₂-ounce) package corn muffin mix
1 egg
¹/₃ cup milk

Heat corn and chili in saucepan; pour into greased 8x12-inch baking dish. Lightly combine muffin mix, egg and milk. Spread as evenly as possible over chili. Mixture will be thin, but it does puff up and fill in. Bake at 450° for 15 minutes or until golden brown. Makes 4 to 6 servings.

SALISBURY STEAK

1¹/₂ pounds lean ground beef
³/₄ cup quick cooking oats
¹/₄ cup finely chopped onions
1 egg, beaten
¹/₂ cup tomato juice
Salt and pepper to taste

Combine ingredients in large mixing bowl; stir gently to mix. Shape into 4 thick oval patties. Place on broiler rack and cook to desired doneness, turning once. Makes 4 servings.
TIP: If desired, cook on outdoor grill and serve with a mushroom sauce. For Inflation Filet Mignon, wrap 1 slice of bacon around each patty before cooking. Serve with baked potato and tossed green salad.

BEEFY RICE CASSEROLE

1¹/₂ pounds lean ground beef
¹/₂ cup chopped onion
1¹/₂ cups uncooked long grain rice
1 can cream of mushroom soup
1 can cream of celery soup
2 soup cans water

Brown ground beef and onion; drain off fat. Put in greased 2-quart casserole. Add rice. Combine soups in mixing bowl; gradually stir in water until blended and smooth. Pour over rice mixture. Bake at 350° for 1 hour and 15 minutes or until liquid is absorbed and rice is tender. Makes 6 to 8 servings.

QUICK HAMBURGER STEW   TOP OF STOVE

> 1 pound lean ground beef
> 1 can vegetarian vegetable soup, undiluted

Brown ground beef; drain off fat. Add soup and simmer 10 minutes.
Makes 4 servings.
TIP: Can serve with or over mashed potatoes, noodles or rice. Kids
enjoy it served on hamburger buns along with carrot sticks and juice.
(Drain off any excess liquid.)

LAYERED HAMBURGER BAKE   OVEN

> 2 pounds lean ground beef
> Prepared mustard
> Salt and pepper
> Thin onion slices
> Sliced tomatoes
> Sliced green pepper rings

Pat half of ground beef in deep 8 or 9-inch round cake pan. Spread with
a little mustard; sprinkle with salt and pepper. Cover meat with onion
slices. Top with tomato slices, then green pepper rings. Pat remaining
ground beef evenly over top. Arrange additional tomato slices over
ground beef. Bake at 350° for 30 minutes or until cooked to desired
doneness. Makes 6 servings.
TIP: If a smaller or larger recipe is desired, decrease or increase
ingredients and size of pan accordingly.

BUSY DAY MEATLOAF   OVEN

> 2 pounds lean ground beef
> 1 envelope Italian salad dressing mix
> 2 eggs, slightly beaten
> $1/3$ cup finely chopped green pepper
> $1/2$ cup soft bread crumbs
> 4 slices lean bacon

Combine first 5 ingredients; shape into loaf in greased shallow baking
dish. Top with bacon slices. Bake at 350° for about 1 hour. Makes 6
servings.
TIP: Serve with mashed potatoes, Stir-Fry Asparagus, Peachy Fruit
Salad, Whole Wheat Muffins and Brownie Cupcakes.

QUICK BEEF LOAF

OVEN

> 1¹/₂ pounds lean ground beef
> 1¹/₂ teaspoons salt
> ¹/₄ teaspoon pepper
> ¹/₂ cup oats
> ¹/₄ cup milk
> 1 egg

Combine ingredients and shape into loaf in greased shallow baking pan. Bake at 350° for 45 to 60 minutes. Makes 6 servings.
TIP: Serve with mashed potatoes, broccoli and molded fruit salad.

BURGOO

TOP OF STOVE

This makes a very good camping recipe, or for serving large groups of people, especially children. Does not freeze well.

> 2 pounds lean ground beef
> 1 can chili beef soup
> 1 can tomato soup
> 1 can vegetarian vegetable soup
> 1 soup can water
> 1 pound elbow macaroni, cooked

Brown ground beef in large pot or Dutch oven; drain. Stir in soups and water. Cook until mixture is heated through. Stir in macaroni and cook 5 minutes. Makes 10 servings.

BASIC MEATBALLS

OVEN

> 3 pounds lean ground beef
> 3 eggs, beaten slightly
> ¹/₂ cup milk
> 4 slices bread (break up)
> ¹/₂ cup finely chopped onion
> Salt and pepper

Combine ingredients. Chill mixture if too soft to form into balls. Shape into desired size meatballs and place on jelly roll pan. Bake at 425° for 15 to 20 minutes or until nicely browned. Remove from baking sheet and use as desired. Makes 6 dozen small meatballs.
TIP: Use for spaghetti, stroganoff, appetizers, etc. Meatballs may be frozen before or after baking. If more seasoning is desired, add parsley, basil, oregano or thyme.

CHILI WITHOUT BEANS   TOP OF STOVE

> 2 pounds lean ground beef
> 1 medium onion, finely chopped
> 4 teaspoons chili powder
> 1 garlic clove, minced
> $^1/_2$ teaspoon oregano, crushed fine
> 2 (16-ounce) cans tomatoes (with liquid)

Brown ground beef and onions; drain. Stir in chili powder, garlic and oregano. Chop tomatoes and add along with juice. Simmer 2 to 3 hours. Makes 4 to 6 servings.
TIP: If you, like me, are a beans with chili fan, add 1 (16-ounce) can kidney beans, drained.

HAMBURGER CHILI DISH   TOP OF STOVE

> 1 pound lean ground beef
> 2 cups coarsely chopped onion
> 1 (14$^1/_2$-ounce) can stewed tomatoes with liquid
> 2 teaspoons chili powder
> 1 teaspoon salt
> $^1/_2$ cup uncooked rice

In large skillet, lightly brown ground beef and onion. Add tomatoes (cut up, if too large) and remaining ingredients. Add 1 cup water. Bring to a boil; reduce heat and simmer, covered, 30 minutes. Uncover; cook 10 minutes or until most of the liquid is absorbed. Makes 4 servings.
TIP: Recipe can be baked in the oven, if desired, at 350° for about the same amount of time.

CHILI BAKE   OVEN

An interesting way to serve chili.

> $^1/_3$ cup butter or margarine
> 5 eggs, lightly beaten
> $^1/_2$ cup yellow cornmeal
> $^3/_4$ cup flour
> 1$^1/_4$ cups milk
> 2 (15-ounce) cans chili with beans

Place butter in a 10-inch cast-iron or oven-proof skillet. Place in 425° oven to melt butter. Meanwhile, combine eggs, cornmeal, flour and milk until smooth. Remove skillet from oven. Carefully pour batter into pan. Spoon chili into center leaving about a 1 $^1/_2$-inch margin around the edge. Bake 18 to 20 minutes, or until puffed and lightly browned. Serve right away. Makes 6 servings.

CHILI BOWL

Try something a little different for a nice change.

For each serving:
Small round loaf bread, unsliced
Melted butter
Homemade or canned chili, heated
Chopped onion
Grated Cheddar cheese
Sour cream

Cut lid from each loaf of bread. Remove three-fourths of bread from center making a bowl. Brush inside of bowl with melted butter. Bake at 350° for 6 minutes, to heat and toast bread a little. Remove from oven. Fill with hot chili. Sprinkle with onion and cheese. Top with sour cream.

ENCHILADA CASSEROLE

2 (16-ounce) cans chili with beans
2 cups regular size corn chips
1 small onion, chopped
1 cup grated Cheddar cheese

In greased 1 1/2-quart casserole, alternate layers of chili, corn chips and chopped onion. Top with grated cheese. Bake at 350° for 30 minutes or until heated through. Makes 6 servings.
TIP: A good meat stretcher. Serve with fruit salad and bread.

COMPANY BEEF CASSEROLE

A lasagne type casserole that will be a favorite for family meals as well as company.

1¹/₂ pounds lean ground beef
1 (15¹/₂-ounce) jar spaghetti sauce
12 ounces small egg noodles
1 (3-ounce) package cream cheese, softened
1 cup sour cream
16 ounces Mozzarella cheese, grated

Brown ground beef; drain off fat. Add spaghetti sauce; simmer 20 minutes. Meanwhile, cook noodles; drain. Beat cream cheese until smooth. Add sour cream; mix well. Spread half the noodles in greased 9x13-inch baking dish. Cover with half the cream cheese mixture; top with half the grated cheese. Spread all the meat sauce over cheese. Layer remaining noodles, cream cheese mixture and grated cheese. Bake at 350° for 30 minutes or until heated through. Makes 12 servings.

KIDNEY BEAN CASSEROLE

TOP OF STOVE
OVEN

1 pound lean ground beef
1 small onion, finely chopped
1 (16-ounce) can kidney beans, drained
1 can cream of mushroom soup
1 cup (4-ounces) grated Cheddar cheese

Lightly brown ground beef and onion; drain. Add kidney beans and soup. Pour into greased 1-quart casserole. Top with grated cheese. Bake at 350° for 45 minutes or until heated through. Makes 4 servings.

BAKED POTATOES HAMBURGER TOPPING

OVEN
TOP OF STOVE

4 large potatoes
$3/4$ pound lean ground beef
2 green onions, sliced
Salt and pepper to taste
$1/2$ cup sour cream
Butter or margarine

Bake potatoes at 400° for 60 minutes or until done. Meanwhile, brown ground beef and onion; drain off all fat. Add salt, pepper and sour cream. Heat to a simmer, but do not boil. Split potatoes and add butter. Top with hamburger topping. Makes 4 servings.

SLOPPY JOES

TOP OF STOVE

2 pounds lean ground beef
$1/4$ cup chopped onions
$1/3$ cup chopped green peppers
1 (15-ounce) can stewed tomatoes, with liquid, chopped
$1/3$ cup catsup
1 tablespoon dry mustard

Combine first 3 ingredients and cook until meat is lightly browned; drain off fat. Add remaining ingredients. Simmer about 15 minutes or until most of the liquid is absorbed. Serve on hamburger buns or over hot dogs. Makes 6 to 8 servings.

HAMBURGERS WITH ONION

> 1 pound lean ground beef
> $^1/_2$ cup fresh bread crumbs
> 1 teaspoon salt
> $^1/_8$ teaspoon pepper
> $^1/_3$ cup butter or margarine
> 2 large onions, thinly sliced

Combine ground beef, bread crumbs, salt and pepper. Shape into 4 oval patties. Melt 3 tablespoons butter in large skillet; add onion and cook until tender and lightly browned. If desired season with salt. Remove and keep warm. Add remaining butter to skillet; add meat patties and cook to desired degree of doneness. Arrange on serving dish and top with onions. Makes 4 servings.
TIP: If desired, serve on hamburger buns.

DINNER NACHOS

> $^3/_4$ pound lean ground beef
> $^1/_3$ cup taco sauce
> 4 cups tortilla chips
> 1 small tomato, chopped coarse
> $^1/_3$ cup sliced ripe olives
> 2 cups (8-ounces) grated Cheddar cheese

Lightly brown ground beef; drain off fat. Add taco sauce. Spread tortilla chips on 12-inch pizza pan or large baking sheet. Spoon meat over top. Sprinkle with tomato, olives and then cheese. Bake at 400° for 10 minutes or until cheese melts. Serves 2 for dinner; 4 for snacks.

TACOS

1 pound lean ground beef
1 (1¼-ounce) package taco seasoning mix
6-8 taco shells or corn tortillas, cooked
Grated Cheddar cheese
Shredded lettuce
Salsa

Brown ground beef; drain. Add seasoning mix and ³/₄ cup water. Reduce heat; simmer about 15 minutes or until liquid is absorbed. Spoon filling into taco shells, sprinkle with grated cheese and lettuce. Top with salsa. Makes about 8 tacos.

DEEP DISH PIZZA

3 cups Bisquick mix
³/₄ cup cold water
1½ pounds lean ground beef
½ cup finely chopped onion
1 (14-ounce) jar pizza sauce or spaghetti sauce
1 (12-ounce) package Mozzarella cheese, grated

Mix Bisquick and water until soft dough forms; beat 20 strokes. Place on floured board and knead about 20 times. With floured hands, press dough evenly on bottom and up sides of greased 11x15-inch jelly roll pan. Lightly brown ground beef and onion; drain off fat. Spread pizza sauce over dough. Distribute meat over top. Sprinkle with grated cheese. Bake at 425° for about 20 minutes or until lightly browned. Watch cheese carefully the last 5 minutes. Makes 6 to 8 servings.
TIP: Use your choice of meat, sliced mushrooms, olives and green onion, if desired.

POPOVER PIZZA

1 pound Italian sausage (or ground beef)
2 cups pizza or spaghetti sauce
1 (12-ounce) package Mozzarella cheese, grated
1 cup flour
1 cup milk
2 eggs

In medium skillet, lightly brown sausage; drain off fat. Add sauce and bring to a boil. Lower heat; cook 2 to 3 minutes. Pour into greased 9x13-inch baking pan. Sprinkle cheese over top. Combine flour, milk and eggs; mix well. Pour over cheese. Bake at 425° for 25 to 30 minutes or until heated through. Makes 6 servings.

REUBEN BURGERS
BROIL

$1^1/_4$ **pounds lean ground beef**
$^1/_2$ **teaspoon seasoning salt**
French bread
Butter or margarine
1 cup sauerkraut, drained
4 slices Swiss cheese

Combine ground beef and salt. Shape into 4 oblong patties and broil to desired doneness. Cut French bread slices, about 1-inch thick, to fit ground beef. Butter and toast bread. Top with beef patty and sauerkraut. Place cheese slices over top and broil to melt cheese. Makes 4 servings.
VARIATION: To make a sandwich, slice bread thinner and top with second slice of bread.

GROUND BEEF DELUXE
BROIL OR GRILL

1 pound lean ground beef
1 teaspoon salt
$^1/_8$ **teaspoon pepper**
4 tomato slices
4 strips of bacon, cooked and crumbled
4 slices cheese

Season ground beef with salt and pepper. Shape into 4 patties. Broil or grill on both sides until browned. Top each with a tomato slice, sprinkle with bacon and top with a cheese slice. Continue cooking until cheese is melted. Makes 4 servings.

HAMBURGERS WITH ALMONDS
BROIL OR GRILL

1 pound lean ground beef
$^1/_4$ **cup slivered almonds, toasted**
$^1/_4$ **teaspoon fine herbs**
1 teaspoon salt
$^1/_8$ **teaspoon pepper**

Combine all ingredients and form into 3 to 4 round patties. Broil or grill to desired doneness. Makes 3 to 4 servings.
TIP: Serve on hamburger buns or toasted buttered French bread, or serve plain meat patties with boiled potatoes, vegetable and salad.

GOURMET BEEF PATTIES

BROIL

1^{1}/$_{2}$ pounds lean ground beef
1^{1}/$_{2}$ teaspoons salt
^{1}/$_{4}$ teaspoon pepper
2 tablespoons ice water
4 thin slices Swiss cheese
4 thin slices cooked ham

Lightly mix ground beef with salt, pepper and ice water. Shape into 8 equal size patties. Place a slice of cheese and ham on 4 patties. Cover with remaining patties; press to seal in ham and cheese. Broil 4 minutes on each side or to desired degree of doneness. Makes 4 servings.

BURGER TOWERS

TOP OF STOVE
GRILL

2 pounds lean ground beef
1 teaspoon seasoned salt
2 large tomatoes
1 (4-ounce) can mushroom caps, drained
2 tablespoons butter
3 split hamburger buns, toasted

Lightly mix ground beef with salt. Shape into 6 patties about 1-inch thick. Pan-fry or grill over medium heat, cooking to desired doneness. Meanwhile, cut each tomato into 3 thick slices. Sauté mushrooms in butter until heated through. Place a meat patty on each bun half; top with tomato slice and garnish with mushroom caps. Makes 6 servings.

BEEF STROGANOFF

TOP OF STOVE

1^{1}/$_{2}$ pounds beef tenderloin or sirloin
6 tablespoons butter or margarine, divided
1 cup chopped onion
4 tablespoons flour
1^{3}/$_{4}$ cups chicken or beef broth
1 cup sour cream

Cut meat across the grain into ^{1}/$_{2}$-inch strips, about 1^{1}/$_{2}$-inches long. Melt 2 tablespoons butter in large skillet. Add onion and cook until tender. Remove onion and set aside. Add remaining butter to skillet. Add half the meat and brown lightly. Remove from skillet. Brown remaining meat. Return all the meat to the skillet, but do not drain off fat. Add flour to skillet and stir to mix. Slowly add broth, stirring until smooth. Cook until thickened, stirring occasionally. Reduce heat. Add sour cream and heat, but do not let boil. Makes 4 servings.
TIP: Serve over rice or noodles.

COMPANY BEEF FILLETS

Beef fillets, 1-1½ inches thick
Butter (Clarified, if possible)
Salt and pepper

Heat butter in heavy skillet until hot. Quickly brown steaks on both sides. Remove from skillet and place in shallow baking pan (do not crowd steaks, they should not be touching). Let stand at room temperature. When ready to cook, bake at 325° for 15 to 18 minutes for medium-rare, about 18 to 22 minutes for medium. Season with salt and pepper.
TIP: A great way to cook steaks for a crowd.

STEAK AU POIVRE

2 New York cut steaks, about 1½ inches thick
2 tablespoons black peppercorns, coarsely ground
1 teaspoon salt
3 tablespoons butter
3 tablespoons oil
⅓ cup cognac

Sprinkle both sides of steak with 1½ teaspoons peppercorns. Press pepper into the meat. Let stand 15 to 20 minutes. Sprinkle one side of steak with salt. Heat butter and oil in skillet over medium-high heat. Place steaks, salted side down, in the hot oil and cook for 3 minutes. Salt steaks, turn, and cook 3 minutes. Reduce heat to medium; cook about 3 minutes on each side. Remove steaks and keep warm. Remove pan from heat, pour in cognac and ignite; pour over steaks.
TIP: For a richer sauce, add a little cream along with the cognac.

BEEF JERKY

Cheaper and better than store bought.

1 flank steak
½ cup soy sauce
½ teaspoon garlic powder
1 teaspoon lemon pepper

Cut flank steak lengthwise (with the grain) in long thin strips no more than ¼ inch thick. Combine remaining ingredients in mixing bowl. Add meat; marinate 1 hour. Baste occasionally if meat is not completely covered with sauce. Arrange meat strips on rack; place on cookie sheet. Bake at 150° for 12 hours. The time can vary a little depending on how your oven bakes. Cool and store in a covered container.

BROILED STEAK

BROIL

1 sirloin steak, 1½ inches thick
1 tablespoon Worcestershire sauce
¼ cup butter, melted
1 teaspoon salt
⅛ teaspoon pepper
½ teaspoon garlic powder

Place steak on rack in roasting pan. Combine remaining ingredients. Brush steaks generously with the sauce. Broil about 3½-inches from broiling unit 9 to 10 minutes. Turn steak, brush with sauce and broil 9 to 10 minutes. This is for medium rare. Cook longer on each side, if desired. Transfer to hot serving platter; pour remaining butter sauce over top. Makes 4 to 6 servings.
TIP: Serve with Swiss Au Gratin Potatoes, Company Baked Carrots, Italian Salad and hard rolls.

STEAK AND ONIONS

TOP OF STOVE

1 pound sirloin steak
4 tablespoons oil, divided
2 large onions, sliced, separated into rings
2 tablespoons soy sauce, divided
2 tablespoons dry sherry, divided
2 tablespoons cornstarch

Cut steak, across the grain, into ⅛-inch slices. Heat 2 tablespoons oil in skillet. Add onion slices and cook 4 to 5 minutes. Stir in 1 tablespoon soy sauce and 1 tablespoon sherry. Cook until onions are beginning to soften but are still crisp. Remove from skillet. Toss steak with remaining soy sauce, sherry and the cornstarch. Heat remaining oil in same skillet. Brown steak. Return onions and cook about 2 minutes to heat through. Makes 4 servings.
TIP: Very good served over rice. Don't overcook the onions, you want them to be crisp cooked, not limp.

KID'S FAVORITE FLANK STEAK

MARINATE
BROIL OR
GRILL

1 flank steak
¼ cup soy sauce

Pour enough soy sauce in shallow dish to cover bottom. Add flank steak and marinate 60 minutes, turning steak frequently. Remove from marinade and broil or grill. Do not overcook as this tends to toughen meat. Slice crosswise to serve. Makes 4 servings.
TIP: For variety, add ¼ cup pineapple juice.

STEAK WITH MUSHROOM SAUCE   Top of Stove

If you want to impress your guest, you can flame the brandy after adding it to the skillet.

> 2 New York steaks
> 1/4 cup butter
> 1/2 cup chopped onion
> 8 mushrooms, sliced
> 2 teaspoons Worcestershire sauce
> 2 tablespoons brandy

Melt butter in large skillet. Brown steak quickly on one side. Reduce heat; add onion and mushrooms. Cook 2 minutes. Turn steaks and cook about 6 minutes or to desired doneness. Add Worcestershire sauce and brandy. Cook about 2 minutes. Makes 2 servings.
TIP: Serve with Green Beans Dijon, rice, salad, and sour dough bread.

TERIYAKI STEAK   Marinate
Broil

> 2 to 3 pound flank steak
> 1 cup firmly packed light brown sugar
> 1 cup soy sauce
> 5 slices fresh ginger
> 1 garlic clove, minced
> 1/2 cup pineapple juice

Place steak in shallow flat dish. Combine remaining ingredients and pour over top. Marinate at least 2 hours at room temperature or refrigerate overnight. Broil or grill to desired doneness, basting frequently with marinade. Makes 4 servings.
TIP: Serve with Honey Glazed Carrots, Au Gratin Potatoes, Honey-Mustard Salad and Sally Lunn Muffins.

SWISS STEAK   Top of Stove
Oven

> 2 pounds round steak, 1 inch thick
> 1/4 cup flour
> Salt and pepper
> 3 tablespoons oil
> 1/2 cup chopped onion
> 1 (16-ounce) can tomatoes, with juice, cut up

Combine flour, salt and pepper; pound into meat. Brown meat on both sides in hot oil in large Dutch oven or skillet. Top with onion and tomatoes. Bake, covered, at 350° for 1 3/4 hours or until tender. Add water if necessary. Makes 4 to 6 servings.
TIP: If desired, add 1/4 cup chopped green peppers the last 15 minutes.

STUFFED FLANK STEAK   OVEN

For a two ingredient recipe, this one has a lot of flavor.

1 to 1^1/₂-pound flank steak
³/₄ pound bulk Italian sausage

Place steak on waxed paper, rounded side down. Pound to flatten slightly. Crumble sausage over steak to within 1 inch of edges. Starting with short end, tightly roll meat. Tie with string (or dental floss) in 5 to 6 places, making sure ends are tied to enclose filling. String should be tight, making a compact loaf. Place seam side down on rack in roasting pan. Bake at 350° for 75 to 85 minutes or until meat and sausage are cooked through. Slice into ¹/₄-inch slices to serve. Makes 6 servings. TIP: Thinly sliced leftover steak makes a delicious sandwich.

FOOL PROOF RIB ROAST   OVEN

1 standing rib roast, 4 pounds or more

Bring beef to room temperature. Place rib side down, on rack, in shallow roasting pan. Roast for 1 hour at 375°. Turn off oven, but do not open door. Leave roast in oven. Approximately an hour before dinner, turn oven on to 375° and roast 30 minutes to an hour longer, depending on size of roast and degree of doneness desired (30 minutes for medium rare). Remove to hot platter and let stand 15 minutes before carving. TIP: Start roast around 11:00 a.m. for dinner. For roast of more than 10 pounds, the final roasting time should be increased 1 hour. Use meat thermometer to check degree of doneness, as oven temperatures and room temperature of the meat can make a difference. Serve with Steamed New Potatoes, Green Beans Supreme, Poppy Seed French Bread and Crisp Green Salad.

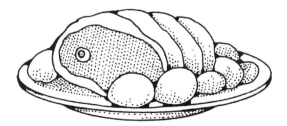

STANDING RIB ROAST   OVEN

1 standing rib roast (4 ribs)

Place beef, rib side down, on rack in shallow roasting pan. Insert meat thermometer so tip is in center of roast. Bake at 325° to desired degree of doneness. The roast will continue to cook internally after removing form oven. Remove from oven when thermometer reads:

Rare	remove at 120° (15-17 minutes per pound)
Medium Rare	remove at 140° (17-20 minutes per pound)
Medium	remove at 150° (20-25 minutes per pound)

Cover with foil and let roast stand 20 minutes before carving. Allow $^3/_4$-1 pound per person.

BASIC POT ROAST   TOP OF STOVE
                                                          OVEN

Serve with boiled potatoes, carrots and tossed salad.

3 to 4 pound rump, chunk or round beef
Flour
$^1/_4$ cup oil
1 large onion, cut into large wedges
Salt and pepper to taste
$1^1/_2$ teaspoons of thyme or an herb blend

Heat oil in heavy pot or Dutch oven. Rub roast with flour. Brown meat slowly in hot oil, turning to brown all sides. Add remaining ingredients along with about 1 cup water. Cover and bake at 350° for about 2 to $2^1/_2$ hours or until meat is tender. Add more water if necessary. If desired,potatoes and carrots can be added last half hour of cooking time. Makes 6 to 8 servings.
TIP: To make gravy see Roast Pan Gravy.

ROLLED RUMP ROAST   OVEN

Rump roast, boned and rolled (use top grades for roasting)
Salt and pepper

Place meat, fat side up, on rack in shallow roasting pan; sprinkle with salt and pepper. Insert meat thermometer; roast, uncovered, at 325° for 2 to $2^1/_2$ hours for a 4 to 6 pound rump roast (150° to 170°). Remove roast from pan; cover and let stand 10 minutes before serving.
TIP: To make AuJus, skim off excess fat from meat juices. Add a little water to pan. Simmer 3 to 4 minutes, stirring to remove crusty pieces. Strain and serve hot.

BEEF FAJITAS

A popular recipe in restaurants as well as home entertaining.

> **1 pound skirt steak, flank steak, or sirloin steak**
> **$^1/_2$ cup fresh lime juice**
> **$^3/_4$ teaspoon garlic salt**
> **$^1/_2$ teaspoon freshly ground black pepper**
> **2 tablespoons oil or butter**
> **Flour tortillas, warmed**

Place beef in shallow dish . Combine next 3 ingredients and pour over meat. Cover and refrigerate several hours or overnight. Remove meat from marinade; drain thoroughly. Brown on grill or in hot oil. Slice diagonally into strips. Serve in warm flour tortillas. Makes 4 servings.
TIP: Chicken breasts halves can be substituted for the beef. Favorite condiments served with Fajitas are, Guacomole, salsa, chopped onion and tomato, or sour cream. One of my favorites is Onions and Peppers.

PEPPER ROAST

Cracked pepper adds a lot of flavor to this tender roast.

> **2 pound sirloin tip roast**
> **$2^1/_2$ teaspoons seasoned salt**
> **3 teaspoons fresh coarsely ground black pepper**

Rub surface of roast evenly with combined salt and pepper mixture. Place on rack in roasting pan. Bake at 350° for 30 minutes per pound or until meat thermometer inserted in center registers 140° for medium rare or 150° for medium. Cover with foil and let stand 15 minutes for easier carving. Makes 4 servings.
TIP: Serve with mashed potatoes, gravy, Company Green Beans and Almond Spinach Salad.

CORNED BEEF CASSEROLE

A quick, from the cupboard, casserole.

> **1 (8-ounce) package wide noodles, cooked, drained**
> **1 (12-ounce) can corned beef, diced**
> **1 cup (4-ounces) grated Cheddar cheese**
> **1 can cream of chicken or mushroom soup**
> **1 cup milk**
> **$^1/_2$ cup finely chopped onion**

Combine last 5 ingredients until blended. Add noodles. Pour into greased 2-quart casserole. Bake at 350° for 45 minutes or until hot. Makes 6 servings.

BUTTERFLIED LAMB

1 leg of lamb, butterflied
2 tablespoons mei yen powder
1 tablespoon bouquet garni for lamb
3 tablespoons red wine vinegar
$^{1}/_{2}$ cup oil

Rub dry ingredients on lamb. Marinate in vinegar and oil for 1 hour, turning occasionally. Broil lamb for 15 minutes on each side or bake at 450° for 45 minutes or until done. Do not overcook, it's okay if lamb is just slightly pink.

TIP: Have butcher butterfly the leg of lamb. The dry ingredients may be purchased in most speciality food shops. If desired, cook on outdoor grill.

LEG OF LAMB

3 to 4 pound leg of lamb, room temperature
Flour
Salt and pepper

Rub leg of lamb with a little flour, salt and pepper. Place on rack and bake at 325° for 3 to 3 $^{1}/_{2}$ hours or until meat thermometer registers 170°. Remove from oven and cover with foil to keep hot. Let stand 20 minutes before carving. Makes 6 servings.

TIP: Serve with apple mint jelly.

COMPANY LAMB CHOPS

4 lamb chops, 1$^{1}/_{2}$ inches thick
1 teaspoon salt
$^{1}/_{4}$ teaspoon pepper
3 tablespoons prepared mustard
3 tablespoons honey

Trim fat from chops. Season with salt and pepper. Broil 7 minutes on one side; turn and broil about 6 minutes on other side or to desired degree of doneness. Do not overcook, it's okay if lamb is pink in the center. Combine mustard and honey; spread over chops. Broil 2 minutes longer. Makes 4 servings.

TIP: Serve with Rice Pilaf, Minted Petite Peas, Spinach Salad and hot rolls.

SAUSAGE KABOBS

4 small red potatoes
2 small onions
1 Polish sausage link, cut into 1^1/$_2$-inch chunks
^{1}/$_4$ cup butter or margarine, melted
Salt and pepper to taste

Cut potatoes in half; steam about 15 minutes or until just tender. Boil onions about 4 minutes; cut each into 4 wedges. On each of 4 skewers, alternately thread potatoes, onion and sausage. Grill or broil about 20 minutes or until sausage is cooked and vegetables are tender. Brush frequently with mixture of butter, salt and pepper. Makes 4 servings.

PORK SAUSAGE CASSEROLE

1 cup uncooked rice
1 pound bulk pork sausage
^{1}/$_2$ cup chopped green pepper
^{1}/$_2$ cup chopped onion
^{1}/$_4$ cup slivered almonds
1 can cream of chicken soup

Cook rice while preparing remaining ingredients. Crumble sausage into large skillet; brown lightly. Add green pepper and onion; cook until tender. Drain off fat. Add almonds and soup; stir to blend. Add rice (mixture will be quite thick). Pour into buttered 2-quart casserole. Bake, uncovered, at 350° for 30 minutes or until heated through. Makes 6 servings.

ITALIAN SAUSAGE SPAGHETTI

A delicious spaghetti you can make in about 30 minutes.

1 pound Italian sausage
1 green pepper, cut into small squares
1^1/$_2$ cups coarsely chopped onion
2-2^1/$_2$ cups spaghetti sauce
10 ounces spaghetti (or desired amount)
Grated Parmesan cheese

In large skillet, lightly brown sausage. Add green pepper and onion; cook until soft but not brown. Add spaghetti sauce. Bring to a boil. Lower heat and simmer 10 to 15 minutes. Meanwhile cook spaghetti as directed on package. Serve sauce over spaghetti. Sprinkle with Parmesan cheese. Makes 4 servings.

SWEET 'N SOUR SPARERIBS

TOP OF STOVE
OVEN

4 pounds pork spareribs
$^3/_4$ cup sugar
$^1/_3$ cup white vinegar
$^1/_4$ cup soy sauce
$^2/_3$ cup cold water
3 tablespoons cornstarch

Place spareribs in large pot; cover with water. Bring to a boil and cook 45 minutes; drain. Meanwhile, in small pan, combine sugar, vinegar and soy sauce. Bring to a boil. Gradually stir cold water into cornstarch; blend until smooth. Add to hot mixture. Cook until thickened, stirring occasionally. Place spareribs in large shallow baking pan. Pour sauce over ribs. Bake at 350° for 60 minutes, basting occasionally, until ribs are glazed and tender. Makes 4 servings.
VARIATION: Use apricot nectar for the $^2/_3$ cup water.

OVEN SPARERIBS

TOP OF STOVE
OVEN

3-4 pounds pork spareribs
$^1/_2$ cup catsup
$^1/_2$ cup firmly packed light brown sugar
2 tablespoons Worcestershire sauce
1 tablespoon white vinegar
Dash hot pepper sauce

Cut spareribs in serving size pieces. Place in large pot and cover with water. Bring to a boil and cook gently 45 minutes or until tender; drain. Place ribs in large baking pan. Combine remaining ingredients and spread over ribs. Bake at 350° for 20 to 30 minutes or until browned and heated through. Makes 4 to 6 servings.

OVEN BARBECUED PORK CHOPS

TOP OF STOVE
OVEN

4 pork chops, $1^1/_2$-inches thick
$^1/_2$ cup catsup
$^3/_4$ cup chutney (Major Grey is very good)
$^1/_4$ cup lemon juice
1 tablespoon light brown sugar
2 teaspoons Worcestershire sauce

Place the last five ingredients in a small saucepan. Stir in $^1/_2$ cup water. Bring to a boil, reduce heat and simmer 20 minutes. Place pork chops in a 9x9-inch baking dish. Pour sauce over top. Bake at 350° for about $1^1/_2$ hours or until pork chops are tender, basting occasionally. Makes 4 servings.

PORK CHOPS ROYAL

4 pork chops, 1 inch thick
Salt and pepper
4 thin slices onion
4 thin slices lemon
4 tablespoons catsup
4 tablespoons light brown sugar

Sprinkle pork chops with salt and pepper; place in greased baking dish. Top each chop with an onion slice and lemon slice. Top each with 1 tablespoon of catsup and 1 tablespoon brown sugar. Cover and bake at 350° for 1 hour; uncover and bake 30 minutes or until tender, basting frequently. Makes 4 servings.

COMPANY GLAZED PORK CHOPS

This is one of my most often used company dishes. Garnish with crabapples on pineapples slices and sprigs of parsley. Serve with a rice dish and green peas.

6 loin cut pork chops, 1 inch thick
6 thick onion slices
Salt and cracked pepper
1 chicken bouillon cube, crushed
2 teaspoons prepared mustard
1/4 cup hot water

Trim fat from pork chops. Melt fat in heavy skillet; add pork chops and brown lightly. Place onion slices in single layer in shallow baking pan; top each with a pork chop. Sprinkle with salt and pepper. Combine bouillon cube, mustard and hot water; stir to dissolve. Pour over pork chops. Cover pan with foil. Bake at 350° for 45 minutes or until chops are tender. Place each chop with onion slice on heated serving platter. Makes 6 servings.

ROAST LOIN OF PORK

1 (5-6 pound) pork loin
1 teaspoon crushed rosemary
2 teaspoons seasoned salt
1 teaspoon pepper

Have meat at room temperature. Wipe dry. Place fat side up on rack in roasting pan. Combine seasonings; sprinkle over roast. Bake at 325°, allowing 24 minutes per pound (2 to 2 1/4 hours) or until meat thermometer reads 170°. Makes 6 serving.

BARBECUED PORK TENDERLOIN

1 or 2 pork tenderloins, about 1^1/$_2$ pounds each
3 tablespoons sherry
3 tablespoons soy sauce
^{1}/$_4$ cup honey
2 slices ginger, minced

Place tenderloin in shallow dish. Combine remaining ingredients and pour over meat. Cover and chill several hours or overnight, turning occasionally. Remove meat from marinade and place in baking dish. Cover and bake at 350° for 1^1/$_2$ hours. Uncover and bake 30 minutes, basting occasionally. Cut crosswise into thin slices. Makes 6 servings.

SLICED PARTY HAM

1 (6-pound) pre-cooked ham
1^1/$_2$ cups apricot preserves
Whole cloves

Have butcher slice ham thin and tie with string. Place ham, on rack in shallow roasting pan. Spread apricot preserves over ham; stud with cloves. Bake at 350° for 1 ^{1}/$_2$ hours or until heated through, basting frequently with pan juices. Remove cloves. Makes 15 to 20 servings.
TIP: A favorite way to serve ham to a large group. Serve ham slices hot or cold, buffet style. Garnish with sprigs of parsley and crabapples.

MUSTARD GLAZED HAM

A delicious, but quick and easy recipe for company entertaining.

Precooked boneless ham
^{1}/$_2$ cup firmly packed light brown sugar
^{1}/$_4$ cup orange juice
^{1}/$_2$ teaspoon dry mustard

Place ham on rack, fat side up. Bake at 325° for 20 minutes per pound or until heated through. Meanwhile, combine remaining ingredients. During last 30 minutes of baking time, brush ham generously with glaze. Continue basting every 10 minutes. Let stand 20 minutes before slicing.
TIP: Serve with Swiss Au Gratin Potatoes, Company Baked Carrots, a spinach salad, hot rolls, and Lemon Mousse.

CASHEW HAM BAKE   OVEN

1 large ham slice, 1-inch thick
$^1/_2$ cup orange marmalade
$^1/_4$ cup coarsely chopped cashews

Place ham slice on rack in roasting pan. Bake at 300° for 45 minutes. Spread marmalade over top and sprinkle with cashews. Bake 15 minutes. Makes 4 to 6 servings.
TIP: Serve with buttered peas, Au Gratin Potatoes, and Crisp Green Salad.

FRANKS 'N CORNBREAD   OVEN
                                              TOP OF STOVE

A kind to your budget recipe. Take ingredients along for camping or boating.

1 egg
$^1/_3$ cup milk
1 ($8^1/_2$-ounce) package corn muffin mix
4 frankfurters
$^1/_2$ cup (2-ounces) grated Cheddar cheese
1 (16-ounce) can chili with beans (optional)

Combine first 3 ingredients, mixing lightly. Pour into greased 9-inch baking dish. Cut frankfurters in half lengthwise, but do not cut all the way through. Open flat and place on top of batter, cutting, if necessary, to fit dish. Sprinkle with cheese. Bake at 400° for 15 to 20 minutes or until golden. Meanwhile, heat chili. Cut cornbread into squares. Top each serving with some of the chili. Makes 4 servings.

PIGS IN BLANKETS   OVEN

Surprise your family with a new way to prepare Pigs In Blankets

1 ($17^1/_4$-ounce) package frozen puff pastry, thawed
6 hot dogs
1 cup (4-ounces) Swiss cheese, grated

On a lightly floured surface, unfold the puff pastry. Lay a hot dog on one corner of the puff pastry. Cut just wide enough to hold the hot dog, leaving a $^1/_4$-inch overlap the length of the hot dog and $^1/_2$-inch overlap at each end. Using this as a guide, cut five more pieces the same size. Sprinkle cheese evenly over pastry to $^1/_2$-inch of the edges. Place a hot dog on each pastry. Slightly wet the edges of pastry with cold water. Roll up and seal edge tightly. Place on ungreased baking sheet, seam side down, tucking ends under. Bake at 450° for 12 to 15 minutes or until light golden brown. Makes 6 servings.
TIP: Serve with your favorite condiments: mustard, catsup, etc.

COOKING TIME FOR FISH

Measure fish at its thickest point
Estimate 10 minutes total cooking time per inch

Total cooking time applies to whatever cooking method is being used—baking, broiling, frying, etc. If baking a salmon or other fish and the fish measures 3 inches at its thickest point, bake 30 minutes at 450°. If broiling a steak $1^1/_2$-inches thick, divide the time and broil $7^1/_2$ minutes on each side. Test with a wooden toothpick; if it comes out clean and dry, fish is done.

COMPANY BAKED SALMON   OVEN

Whole salmon, cleaned and wiped dry
Salt and pepper
Bacon slices

Sprinkle inside of salmon with salt. Salt and pepper outside. Place on large sheet of heavy duty foil in shallow baking pan. Place bacon slices inside salmon and crosswise over top. Wrap foil to seal. Bake at 450° for 10 minutes per inch measuring salmon at its thickest point. Test for doneness. If wooden toothpick is dry, salmon is done.
VARIATION: Add lemon slices and onion rings to inside of salmon.

BAKED SALMON   OVEN

$2^1/_2$ pound salmon fillet
Salt and pepper
2 tablespoons fresh lemon juice
1 cup sour cream
2 teaspoons finely chopped onion

Place fillet in shallow baking dish. Season with salt and pepper; sprinkle with lemon juice. Spread sour cream over top; sprinkle with chopped onion. Bake at 450° for 10 minutes per inch measuring at its thickest point. Makes 6 servings.
TIP: Serve with Vegetable Stir Fry, rice, Sweet-Sour Spinach Salad, hot rolls, and Lemon Mousse.

BAKED SALMON STEAKS   OVEN

4 salmon steaks, 1-inch thick
$^1/_3$ cup melted butter
$^1/_2$ teaspoon salt
2 teaspoons Worcestershire sauce

Place salmon steaks in greased shallow baking pan. Combine remaining ingredients; brush salmon with sauce. Bake at 450° for 10 minutes, basting occasionally with sauce. Steaks are done when wooden toothpick inserted comes out clean. Makes 4 servings.
TIP: If desired, cook under broiler or on grill, turning midway between cooking time; baste frequently with sauce.

TERIYAKI SALMON STEAKS   MARINATE
                                                    BROIL

4 salmon steaks, 1-inch thick
$^1/_4$ cup oil
2 tablespoons lemon juice
2 tablespoons soy sauce
$^1/_2$ teaspoon dry mustard
$^1/_2$ teaspoon ground ginger

Place salmon steaks in shallow dish. Combine remaining ingredients; pour over steaks. Let stand at room temperature 1 hour, turning occasionally. Drain, reserving marinade. Place steaks on rack in broiling pan; broil steaks for 5 minutes; turn and brush with marinade. Broil steaks for 5 minutes more, brushing occasionally with the sauce. Check for doneness. Makes 4 servings.

SALMON LOAF   OVEN

1 (14-ounce) can salmon
1 can cream of mushroom soup
$1^1/_2$ cups soft bread crumbs
$^1/_4$ cup finely chopped celery
2 tablespoons finely chopped onion
2 eggs

Combine ingredients and put in greased loaf pan. Bake at 350° for 45 to 50 minutes or until center is firm. Let stand 5 minutes. Turn out on serving plate. Makes 4 to 6 servings.

FILLETS WITH SHRIMP

2 pound fish fillets (white fish)
$^1/_3$ cup butter or margarine
1 can cream of shrimp soup
$^1/_2$ soup can half and half
$^1/_4$ teaspoon tarragon
$^1/_4$ cup dry sherry

Melt butter in large skillet. Brown fillets on both sides, cooking until fish flakes easily. Meanwhile, combine remaining ingredients in saucepan; bring to a boil. Arrange fish on serving dish; top with sauce. Makes 4 to 6 servings.

FRESH CANNED SHRIMP

Shrimp will taste almost as good as fresh.

Canned shrimp
1 teaspoon salt

Drain shrimp; rinse several times. Place shrimp in quart jar; cover with ice water and the 1 teaspoon salt. Chill overnight. Drain shrimp and pat dry with paper towels.
TIP: Use in shrimp cocktail, salads, soups, main dishes, etc.

BACON PRAWNS

Jumbo prawns are so large, you can allow 3 to 4 per person, for a special meal that won't ruin your budget.

Raw Prawns - allow 3 to 4 per person
Bacon - 1 slice per prawn
Melted butter with parsley or desired herbs

Cook bacon until part of the fat has cooked out, but bacon is still very limp; do not allow bacon to brown at all. Drain on paper towels. Shell prawns, except for the tails and devein. Wrap bacon around shrimp; secure with a toothpick. If bacon strip is too long, cut off excess. Place on rack or grill, baste with butter mixture and cook, turning once, until prawns are opaque and turn pink. Brush occasionally with butter mixture.

BUTTERFLIED SHRIMP   TOP OF STOVE

1 pound shrimp
Salt and pepper
1 egg, slightly beaten with 1 tablespoon water
1/2 cup fine dry bread crumbs
Oil

Remove shells from shrimp, leaving tails intact; devein. Cut two-thirds of the way through the center of each shrimp; flatten out. Season with salt and pepper. Dip in crumbs, egg and then again in crumbs. Fry in deep oil (350°) for about 3 minutes or until golden. Drain and serve. Makes 3 servings.
TIP: Serve with tartar sauce, cole slaw and Au Gratin Potatoes.

SKILLET SHRIMP   TOP OF STOVE

2 pounds shrimp, peeled and cleaned
1/3 cup oil
2 small garlic cloves, minced
1 teaspoon salt
1/2 teaspoon pepper
1/4 cup fresh lemon juice

Heat oil in large skillet. Stir in garlic, salt, pepper and lemon juice. Add shrimp. Cook until shrimp turns pink. Reduce heat and cook until liquid is almost absorbed (do not overcook shrimp). Serve hot. Makes 4 to 6 servings.
TIP: For added color, sprinkle with chopped parsley or garnish dish with parsley sprigs.

SAUTÉED SHRIMP   TOP OF STOVE

24 large shrimp
1/2 cup flour
1/2 cup butter
Juice of 1 lemon
Salt and pepper

Peel and split shrimp. Roll in flour; shake off excess. Heat butter in large skillet. Add shrimp and sauté until lightly browned. Sprinkle with lemon juice, salt and pepper. Makes 4 servings.

CRABMEAT SKILLET   TOP OF STOVE

    1 pound fresh crabmeat, lump style
    $^1/_4$ cup butter
    1 tablespoon chopped green onion
    2 tablespoons tarragon vinegar
    1 teaspoon Worcestershire sauce
    Salt and pepper to taste

Melt butter in skillet. Add crabmeat and saute' a few minutes. Add remaining ingredients; heat through. Serve immediately. Makes 3 to 4 servings.

QUICK CRAB CAKES   TOP OF STOVE

    2 cups flaked crab meat
    1 tablespoon lemon juice
    1 egg, beaten
    Salt and pepper to taste
    1 cup fine bread crumbs, plus extra
    Oil

Combine first 5 ingredients in mixing bowl; mix well. If mixture is too wet, add more bread crumbs, if too dry, add a little water. Shape into 6 patties; dip in additional bread crumbs. Brown lightly on both sides in hot oil. Makes 3 servings.

CRAB SEAFOOD CASSEROLE   OVEN

    1 ($6^1/_2$-ounce) can crab, drained
    1 can cream of shrimp soup
    $^2/_3$ cup milk
    $^1/_2$ cup mayonnaise
    $^1/_2$ cup (2-ounces) grated Cheddar cheese
    $1^1/_2$ cups ($3^1/_2$-ounces) uncooked egg noodles

Combine ingredients and pour into greased 2-quart casserole. Cover and bake at 350° for 45 minutes. Makes 6 servings.
TIP: Casserole may be sprinkled with buttered bread crumbs, French fried onions or grated cheese before baking.

CRAB DIVAN   OVEN

    1 (6^1/$_2$-ounce) can crab, drained
    1 (10-ounce) package frozen broccoli, cooked and drained
    ^{1}/$_2$ cup mayonnaise
    1 teaspoon prepared mustard
    1 tablespoon finely chopped onion
    ^{1}/$_2$ cup (2-ounces) grated Cheddar cheese

Arrange broccoli in bottom of buttered 1-quart casserole. Distribute crab evenly over top. Combine mayonnaise, mustard and onion; spread over crab. Sprinkle with cheese. Bake at 350° for 20 to 30 minutes or until heated through. Makes 4 servings.

TUNA CASHEW CASSEROLE   OVEN

    1 (6^1/$_2$-ounce) can tuna, drained
    1 can cream of mushroom soup
    1 cup thinly sliced celery
    ^{1}/$_4$ cup finely chopped onion
    1 (3-ounce) can Chow Mein Noodles
    1 (3-ounce) package cashews, split

Combine soup with ^{1}/$_4$ cup water. Add remaining ingredients, reserving ^{1}/$_3$ of the Chow Mein Noodles. Pour mixture into greased 1-quart casserole. Sprinkle reserved noodles over top. Bake at 350° for 30 minutes. Makes 4 to 6 servings.

TUNA RICE CASSEROLE   OVEN

    1 (6^1/$_2$-ounce) can tuna, drained
    1 can cream of mushroom soup
    1 cup cooked rice
    1 small onion, chopped
    1 cup crushed potato chips

Gently combine ingredients until mixed. Put in greased 1-quart casserole. Bake at 350° for 30 to 45 minutes. Makes 4 servings.
TIP: If desired, top casserole with additional crushed potato chips.

TUNA MORNAY

2 (6^1/$_2$-ounce) cans tuna, drained
^{1}/$_4$ cup butter or margarine
^{1}/$_4$ cup flour
2 cups milk
^{1}/$_4$ cup grated Swiss cheese
Salt and pepper

Melt butter in medium saucepan. Stir in flour and cook for about 1 minute. Remove from heat; add milk, stirring to blend. Return to heat, continue cooking, stirring frequently, until thickened. Add grated cheese; stir until melted. Add salt and pepper to taste. Stir in tuna. Makes 4 servings.
TIP: Serve over hot buttered toast, rice or noodles.

QUICK TUNA HOT DISH

1 (6^1/$_2$-ounce) can tuna, drained
1 can cream of chicken soup
^{1}/$_2$ cup milk
1 cup cooked peas
2^1/$_2$ cups crushed potato chips

Combine soup and milk in mixing bowl; mix until smooth. Stir in tuna, peas and 2 cups of the crushed potato chips. Pour into greased 1-quart casserole. Top with remaining ^{1}/$_2$ cup potato chips. Bake at 350° for 30 minutes or until heated through. Makes 4 servings.

TROUT AMANDINE

4 trout (about ^{1}/$_2$-pound each)
^{1}/$_2$ cup melted butter
^{1}/$_3$ cup slivered almonds
1 tablespoon lemon juice

Wipe trout dry with paper towels. Brush both sides with melted butter. Place on buttered broiler pan. Broil 4 inches from heat, about 8 to 10 minutes or until fish test done, being careful not to overcook. (Do not try to turn fish.)
While fish is cooking, brown almonds lightly in remaining butter; add lemon juice. Pour over fish. Makes 4 servings.

MUSHROOM FILLET DISH   OVEN

>2 pounds fillets (white fish)
>1 medium onion, finely chopped
>8 ounces fresh mushrooms, sliced
>1 cup (4-ounces) grated Swiss cheese
>Salt and pepper
>1 cup whipping cream

Sprinkle onion evenly in greased shallow 10x6-inch baking dish. Arrange three-fourths of the mushrooms over onion. Sprinkle with half the grated cheese. Place fillets over the top; sprinkle with salt and pepper. Add remaining mushrooms and cheese. Pour whipping cream over top. Bake at 400° for 20 minutes. Makes 4 to 6 servings.

BAKED HALIBUT   MARINATE
                                                    OVEN

>4 halibut steaks, 1-inch thick
>3 tablespoons fresh lemon juice
>1 teaspoon salt
>$^{1}/_{2}$ teaspoon paprika
>$^{1}/_{2}$ cup chopped onion
>2 tablespoons butter

In shallow dish, combine lemon juice, salt and paprika. Add halibut, turning to coat. Marinate 1 hour, turning steaks after first half hour. Sauté onion in butter until tender. Place halibut in greased 10x6-inch baking dish; top with onion. Bake at 450° for 10 minutes or until fish flakes easily with a fork. Makes 4 servings.

HALIBUT-SHRIMP BAKE   OVEN

A favorite recipe from a local restaurant.

>4 small halibut steaks or fillets
>$^{1}/_{2}$ cup fresh lemon juice
>$^{1}/_{2}$ cup butter, melted
>$^{1}/_{2}$ cup sour cream
>$^{1}/_{2}$ cup (2-ounces) Cheddar cheese
>$^{1}/_{3}$ cup tiny shrimp, cooked

Place halibut in shallow baking pan. Combine butter and lemon juice; pour over halibut. Bake at 350° for 10 to 12 minutes or until fish tests done. Top each steak or fillet with some of the sour cream. Sprinkle with cheese. Place under broiler and cook just until cheese melts. Garnish top with shrimp. Makes 4 servings.

TURKEY   OVEN

Turkey
Oil or melted butter

Place turkey, breast side up, on rack in shallow roasting pan. Brush with oil or butter. Cover loosely with foil (barely touching the turkey). Bake at 325°, basting occasionally with pan drippings, oil or butter.

6-8 pounds	$3^1/_2$-4 hours
8-12 pounds	4-$4^1/_2$ hours
12-16 pounds	$4^1/_2$-$5^1/_2$ hours
16-20 pounds	$5^1/_2$-$6^1/_2$ hours
20-24 pounds	$6^1/_2$-$7^1/_2$ hours

Stuffed turkeys require a slightly longer cooking time (30 to 40 minutes). To assure even browning, remove foil the last 30 minutes of cooking time. Test for doneness. Meat thermometer should read 185° or thickest part of drumstick should move up and down easily. Remove from oven; baste. Cover with foil to keep warm. Let stand 15 minutes before carving. If gravy is desired, see Index.

FOIL-WRAPPED TURKEY   OVEN

Turkey
Wide heavy duty foil
Oil or melted butter

Cut 2 long strips of foil. Place one piece lengthwise in large shallow roasting pan and one piece crosswise in pan. Place turkey, breast side up, on top of foil. Brush with oil or butter. Bring 2 opposite ends of foil up over turkey; fold ends together to seal. Bring remaining two end of foil up and seal. Bake at 450°.

8-10 pounds	$2^1/_4$-$2^1/_2$ hours
10-12 pounds	$2^3/_4$-3 hours
14-16 pounds	3-$3^1/_4$ hours
18-20 pounds	$3^1/_4$-$3^1/_2$ hours
22-24 pounds	$3^1/_2$-$3^3/_4$ hours

For stuffed turkeys you may find it necessary to cook 30 minutes longer. To brown turkey, open foil during last 30 minutes of cooking time. Test for doneness. Meat thermometer should read 185° or thickest part of drumstick should move up and down easily. Close foil and let stand 15 minutes before carving.

TIP: This is my favorite way to bake turkey. Basting is eliminated and it provides lots of turkey stock for gravy. Baking time is much quicker.

CANTONESE CORNISH HENS   OVEN

2 Cornish hens, thawed, halved
$^1/_4$ cup soy sauce
$^1/_4$ cup lemon juice
$^1/_4$ cup honey
$^1/_2$ cup catsup

Arrange cornish hen halves in single layer in large baking dish. Combine remaining ingredients and pour over top. Refrigerate several hours or overnight. Cover with foil and bake at 325° for 30 minutes. Remove foil; bake 30 minutes longer or until tender, basting occasionally. Makes 4 servings.

ROAST CORNISH HENS   OVEN

4 Cornish hens
1 teaspoon seasoned salt
$^1/_4$ teaspoon garlic powder
$^1/_4$ teaspoon paprika

Wash and drain hens but do not dry. Combine last 3 ingredients; sprinkle evenly over hens. Place breast down in buttered shallow baking pan. Bake at 425° for 30 minutes. If hens stick, add a little butter to pan. Turn breast side up and bake 30 to 40 minutes longer or until golden brown and tender, basting occasionally with pan drippings. Makes 4 large servings.
TIP: For variation, brush hens with a mixture of equal parts honey and apricot nectar; brush with additional sauce during baking time.

CORNISH HENS ITALIAN   OVEN

2 Cornish hens
1 cup uncooked long-grain rice
1 envelope Italian salad dressing mix
$2^1/_2$ cups boiling water
1 can cream of chicken soup
Salt and pepper

Spread rice in greased 9x13-inch baking dish. Bake at 375° for 10 to 12 minutes, or until golden (watch carefully). Combine salad dressing mix, water and soup; mix well. Pour over rice. Clean hens; cut in half lengthwise. Place hens, skin-side up, on top of rice. Sprinkle with salt and pepper. Cover dish with foil. Bake at 350° for 60 minutes. Remove foil; bake 30 minutes or until liquid is absorbed and hens are tender. Makes 4 servings.

PINEAPPLE STUFFED CORNISH HENS

 4 Cornish hens, thawed
 $^1/_2$ cup melted butter or margarine, divided
 5 cups seasoned bread cubes for stuffing
 $^1/_2$ cup chopped walnuts
 $^3/_4$ cup crushed pineapple, drained
 1 egg, slightly beaten

Combine $^1/_4$ cup of the butter with $^1/_2$ cup water and remaining ingredients; mix well. Stuff hens. Place on rack in roasting pan and roast at 350° for 60 minutes or until tender, basting occasionally with remaining butter. Makes 4 servings.

FRIED CHICKEN

 1 chicken, cut up
 1 egg
 $^1/_2$ cup milk
 1 cup flour
 Salt and pepper
 Shortening or oil

Wash chicken; pat dry. Combine egg and milk in small dish. Combine flour, salt and pepper. Dip chicken in flour, then in milk mixture, then back in flour. Add 1 inch oil to skillet; heat. When hot, add chicken and brown on both sides. Reduce heat; continue cooking until chicken is tender, about 20 to 30 minutes (do not cover). Turn chicken several times while cooking. Drain on paper towels. Makes 4 servings.

CRUNCHY FRIED CHICKEN

Move over Colonel Sanders!

 1 chicken, cut up
 Salt and pepper
 1-1$^1/_2$ cups flour
 1 cup buttermilk
 Oil

Pat chicken dry with paper towels. Sprinkle chicken with salt and pepper. Coat with flour. Dip in buttermilk and again in flour. Heat about 1$^1/_4$-inches oil in a deep heavy skillet. Cook chicken in hot oil, about 20 to 30 minutes, turning once. Drain on paper towels. Makes 4 servings.

OVEN FRIED CHICKEN   OVEN

    1 chicken, cut up
    $^1/_2$ cup flour
    $1^1/_2$ teaspoons salt
    $^1/_4$ teaspoon pepper
    1 teaspoon paprika
    $^1/_4$ cup oil

Combine dry ingredients. Coat chicken pieces with flour mixture. Pour oil into jelly roll pan. Add chicken, skin-side down. Bake at 400° for 30 minutes. Turn and bake 30 minutes or until tender. If chicken pieces are small, bake 20 minutes on each side. Makes 4 servings.

CHICKEN CORDON BLEU   OVEN

    2 large whole chicken breasts, halved, boned, skinned
    4 thin slices boiled ham, (about 3 inch squares)
    4 small thin slices Swiss cheese
    $^3/_4$ cup fine dry bread crumbs
    Salt and pepper
    $^1/_3$ cup melted butter

Cut a deep pocket in side of each chicken breast at its thickest part. Fold a ham slice around a cheese slice, tuck in pocket. Skewer with tooth-picks to secure. Combine bread crumbs, salt and pepper. Roll chicken in butter, then in bread crumbs. Place on buttered baking sheet. Bake at 400° for 30 to 40 minutes or until lightly browned and tender. If chicken becomes dry, brush with leftover butter. Makes 4 servings.

CANDIED CHICKEN   OVEN

    2 whole chicken breasts, halved
    Salt and pepper
    1 cup maple flavored syrup (Log Cabin)
    $^1/_2$ cup white vinegar
    $^1/_2$ cup catsup
    $^1/_4$ cup packed light brown sugar

Sprinkle chicken with salt and pepper. Place, skin-side down, in 9x13-inch baking pan. Combine remaining ingredients until blended. Pour over chicken. Cover with foil and bake at 325° for $1^1/_2$ hours. Turn chicken. Bake, uncovered, 30 minutes, basting frequently to glaze chicken.
TIP: I suggest serving the chicken on a bed of rice; garnish with sprigs of parsley. Pass the sauce to serve over rice. Delicious.

CHICKEN ELEGANT

4 boned whole chicken breasts
$^1/_3$ cup plus 3 tablespoons butter
1 cup seasoned chicken broth
$^1/_4$ cup flour
1 cup half and half
Salt and pepper

Chicken breasts should be left whole with bones removed (do not remove skin). Heat the $^1/_3$ cup butter in heavy skillet. Tuck chicken breast ends under, shaping into a nice round. Brown bottom side first, turn and brown top side. Place in shallow baking dish. Add chicken broth. Cover with foil and bake at 375° for 60 minutes or until tender. Remove chicken and keep warm (reserve broth). Melt the 3 tablespoons butter in small saucepan; stir in flour until blended. Remove from heat; stir in reserved broth and half and half. Cook, stirring frequently, until mixture boils and thickens. Season to taste with salt and pepper. Place chicken on serving plate; pour sauce over top. Makes 4 servings.
TIP: Serve with fresh cooked broccoli and Almond Rice Casserole with Ice cream Cake for dessert. An elegant dinner menu.

COMPANY CHICKEN AND RICE

6 whole chicken breasts, halved
$1^1/_2$ cups uncooked long-grain rice
1 can cream of celery soup
1 can cream of mushroom soup
1 can cream of chicken soup
$^1/_2$ cup melted butter

Place rice in bottom of large buttered roasting pan (pan should be at least 2-inches deep). Combine soups in mixing bowl; gradually stir in $1^1/_2$ soup cans water, stirring to blend. Pour over rice. Dip chicken in butter; place skin-side up on rice mixture. Bake, uncovered, at 250° for $2^1/_2$ hours or at 350° for $1^1/_2$ hours or until liquid is absorbed, rice is tender and chicken has browned. Makes 12 servings.
TIP: You can add 1 (4-ounce) can sliced mushrooms and/or $^1/_2$ cup slivered almonds. Serve with Spinach Salad, Company Baked Carrots and hot rolls. A favorite buffet dish.

CHICKEN PECAN MOUNDS

OVEN

4 whole chicken breasts
Salt and pepper
3 cups seasoned stuffing mix
$1/2$ cup melted butter or margarine
$1/2$ cup finely chopped pecans
$1/2$ cup water

Salt and pepper chicken; set aside. Combine remaining ingredients. Divide into 4 equal parts. Shape into mounds on baking sheet. Place chicken, skin-side up, over top of stuffing. Cover with foil; bake at 350° for 40 minutes. Remove foil; bake 20 minutes or until chicken is browned and tender. Makes 4 large servings.

SWEET-SOUR CHICKEN

TOP OF STOVE
OVEN

1 chicken, cut up
1 cup catsup
$3/4$ cup white vinegar
$1^1/2$ teaspoons prepared mustard
$1^1/2$ cups firmly packed light brown sugar

Combine last 4 ingredients in small saucepan. Bring to a boil; reduce heat and simmer 30 minutes. Place chicken, skin side-down, in buttered 9x13-inch baking dish. Brush generously with sauce. Bake at 350° for 30 minutes; turn, bake 30 minutes basting frequently with sauce. Makes 4 servings.
TIP: Leftover sauce can be frozen and used for spareribs, pork chops, etc. Serve with rice, broccoli, and hot buttered rolls.

TERIYAKI CHICKEN

MARINATE
OVEN

1 chicken, cut up
2 tablespoons oil
$1/2$ cup soy sauce
1 teaspoon sugar
$1/3$ cup finely chopped onion
1 garlic clove, minced

Combine last 5 ingredients. Pour over chicken; marinate at least 2 hours. Place chicken on rack in baking pan; brush with marinade. Bake at 350° for 60 minutes or until tender, basting occasionally. Makes 4 servings.

GOURMET BAKED CHICKEN

5 whole chicken breasts, halved, boned, skinned
2 cups sour cream
1 tablespoon Worcestershire sauce
2 teaspoons salt
$1^1/_4$ teaspoons paprika
$1^1/_2$ cups fine dry bread crumbs

Place chicken in shallow baking dish. Combine sour cream, Worcestershire sauce, salt and paprika; pour over top. Turn chicken to coat. Cover and refrigerate overnight. Next day, drop chicken pieces, one at a time in bread crumbs, turning to coat. Shape each piece to make a nice round fillet. Place in buttered baking pan. Cover and chill at least $1^1/_2$ hours. Bake at 325° for about $1^1/_4$ hours or until golden and tender. (While baking, if chicken looks dry, baste with a little melted butter.) Makes 10 servings.
TIP: A favorite holiday dish, even good served cold. Serve with Rice Pilaf, Minted Petite Peas, Strawberry Nut Salad and hot rolls.

SUPER CHICKEN

This is one of my favorite variations of this recipe.

1 chicken, cut up
1 (18-ounce) jar apricot preserves
1 (8-ounce) bottle Russian salad dressing
1 envelope dry onion soup mix

Place chicken in greased 9x13-inch baking dish. Combine remaining ingredients; pour over chicken. Bake at 350° for 60 minutes, basting every 15 minutes or so. Makes 4 servings.

EASY PARTY CHICKEN

1 chicken, cut up
1 (16-ounce) can whole berry cranberry sauce
1 (8-ounce) bottle creamy French dressing
1 package onion soup mix

Arrange chicken in 9x13-inch baking dish. Combine remaining ingredients until blended. Pour over chicken. Cover and marinate several hour or overnight, turning once or twice. Bake, uncovered at 400° for 45 to 60 minutes, basting occasionally. Makes 4 servings.

JAPANESE CUTLETS

2 whole chicken breasts, halved, boned, skinned
1 egg
2 tablespoons water
$^1/_3$ cup flour
1 (5-ounce) package Panko
Oil

Place chicken between waxed paper. Pound until meat is about $^3/_8$-inch thick, watching carefully so as not to tear the meat. Combine egg and water. Dip cutlets in flour, then in egg mixture, then in Panko, turning to coat evenly. Fry in hot oil in skillet until golden, turning to brown other side. Makes 4 servings.
TIP: Panko is a dry Japanese breading that can be found in the Oriental food section of most grocery stores.

CHINESE BROWNED CHICKEN

Another "so easy" recipe.

2 whole chicken breasts, halved (or 1 chicken, cut up)
2 tablespoons melted butter or margarine
2 tablespoons Worcestershire sauce
1 tablespoon soy sauce

Line baking pan with foil for easier cleaning. Place chicken on foil, skin-side up. Combine remaining ingredients. Brush chicken with mixture; bake at 350° for 60 minutes, basting occasionally with butter mixture and pan juices. Makes 4 servings.

MOZZARELLA CHICKEN BAKE

2 large chicken breasts, halved, boned, skinned
$^1/_3$ cup flour
$^1/_4$ cup butter
Salt and pepper
4 large mushrooms, sliced
4 rectangle slices Mozzarella cheese

Place chicken halves between waxed paper and pound thin, being careful not to tear chicken. Coat with flour. Heat butter in skillet; add chicken and cook until tender, about 4 to 5 minutes on each side. Place chicken on broiler pan; sprinkle with salt and pepper. Quickly sauté mushrooms in skillet; arrange slices on chicken. Top with slice of cheese. Place under broiler just long enough to melt cheese. Makes 4 servings.

CHICKEN COCONUT

> **2 whole chicken breasts, halved**
> **Salt and pepper**
> **Oil**
> **$^1/_3$ cup fine dry bread crumbs**
> **$^1/_3$ cup Angel Flake coconut**
> **$^1/_4$ cup melted butter**

Sprinkle chicken with salt and pepper. Brush with oil. Combine bread crumbs and coconut. Roll chicken in mixture to coat. Place in greased shallow baking pan; drizzle melted butter over top. Bake at 350° for 40 minutes or until tender. Makes 4 servings.

PEACHY CHICKEN

> **1 chicken, cut up**
> **1 (29-ounce) can peach halves, save juice**
> **$^1/_4$ cup soy sauce**

Arrange chicken, skin-side down, in buttered 9x13-inch baking dish. Combine peach syrup with soy sauce. Pour over chicken. Bake at 350° for 30 minutes. Turn chicken, bake 30 minutes, basting frequently, until tender. Serve peaches with chicken. Makes 4 servings.
TIP: Peach halves can be heated along with chicken the last 10 minutes of baking time.

RITZ BAKED CHICKEN

> **2 whole chicken breasts, halved**
> **$^1/_2$ cup sour cream**
> **1 tablespoon Worcestershire sauce**
> **1 tablespoon lemon juice**
> **1 cup crushed Ritz crackers**

Combine sour cream, Worcestershire sauce and lemon juice. Dip chicken in mixture; roll in cracker crumbs. Place on baking sheet and bake at 325° for 45 to 60 minutes or until tender. Makes 4 servings.

GINGER BAKED CHICKEN   OVEN

1 chicken, cut up
$^1/_2$ cup soy sauce
$^1/_2$ cup white wine
$^1/_2$ cup orange juice
$^1/_4$ teaspoon garlic powder
$^1/_4$ teaspoon ground ginger

Combine last 5 ingredients. Pour over chicken and marinate at least 60 minutes, turning chicken occasionally. Place chicken, skin-side down, in greased 9x13-inch baking dish. Bake at 350° for 30 minutes. Turn chicken and bake 30 minutes or until tender, basting frequently with sauce. Makes 4 servings.
TIP: Serve with Almond Rice Casserole, Mushroom Salad, green beans and hot rolls.

QUICK CHICKEN DIVAN   OVEN

1 pound fresh broccoli, cooked
4 large slices cooked chicken or turkey (or several smaller)
1 can cream of chicken soup
$^1/_3$ cup milk
$^1/_2$ cup grated Cheddar cheese

Place broccoli in greased 10x7-inch baking dish. Top with chicken slices. Combine soup and milk until blended. Pour over chicken. Sprinkle with cheese. Bake at 350° for 30 minutes. Makes 4 servings.

CHINESE NOODLE CASSEROLE   OVEN

1$^1/_2$ cups diced cooked chicken
1 cup finely chopped celery
1 cup cashews, split
2 cans cream of mushroom soup
1 cup chicken broth (or water)
1 (5-ounce) can Chow Mein Noodles

Combine chicken, celery, and cashews in mixing bowl. Combine soup and broth until blended. Pour over chicken mixture; stir to mix. Layer in greased 2-quart deep casserole, starting with half of the chicken mixture, then half the noodles. Repeat ending with noodles. Bake at 350° for 45 minutes or until heated through. Makes 6 servings.
TIP: If a little onion is desired, add $^1/_3$ cup, finely chopped. This is best served hot from the oven as Chow Mein Noodles tend to soften when reheated.

SHOPPERS CHICKEN

> 3 whole chicken breasts, halved
> 1 cup sour cream
> 2 tablespoons lemon juice
> 1 teaspoon salt
> 1 teaspoon paprika
> $^1/_2$ cup melted butter or margarine

Combine sour cream, lemon juice, salt and paprika. Place chicken, skin-side up, in buttered 9x13-inch baking dish. Spread mixture over top. Pour butter over chicken. Bake at 350° for 60 minutes. Makes 6 servings.

BAKED CHICKEN CURRY

> 1 chicken, cut up
> $^1/_2$ cup butter or margarine, melted
> 1 teaspoon lemon juice
> 2 cloves garlic, minced
> 1 teaspoon salt
> 2 teaspoons curry powder

Place chicken, skin-side down, in greased 9x13-inch baking dish. Combine remaining ingredients. Brush chicken with some of the sauce. Bake at 350° for 30 minutes, basting once. Turn chicken, bake 30 minutes, basting with additional sauce every 10 minutes until chicken is tender. Makes 4 servings.

CHICKEN TARRAGON

> 3 whole chicken breasts, skinned, and boned
> 4 tablespoons butter or margarine
> $1^1/_2$ teaspoons flour
> $^1/_2$ cup Vermouth
> $^1/_2$ cup sour cream
> $^1/_4$ teaspoon dried tarragon

Heat butter in heavy skillet. Cut chicken into bite-size pieces and lightly brown in skillet. Remove chicken; put in greased 1-quart casserole. Pour off all but one tablespoon butter. Heat butter; stir in flour and mix well. Bring to a boil. Remove from heat; add vermouth; mix until smooth. Add sour cream and tarragon; blend. Pour over chicken. Bake at 350° for 30 minutes. Makes 4 servings.
TIP: Sauce is excellent served over rice, but make $1^1/2$ times the recipe.

SAVORY GRILLED CHICKEN

GRILL

> 1 chicken, cut up
> Seasoned salt
> Butter, melted

Place chicken on large piece of heavy duty foil. Sprinkle generously with salt. Fold foil over and secure tightly. Place on grill and cook 45 minutes turning frequently to avoid burning. Open foil; place chicken directly on grill, turning to brown both sides. Baste with butter. Makes 4 servings.

TIP: Meat is so tender it will literally fall off the bone.

ROQUEFORT CHICKEN

TOP OF STOVE
OVEN

> 3 whole chicken breasts, halved, boned
> Salt and pepper
> 1/4 cup butter
> 4 ounces Roquefort cheese
> 1 garlic clove, minced
> 1 cup sour cream

Salt and pepper chicken. Heat butter in heavy skillet. Lightly brown chicken; remove. In skillet, add Roquefort, garlic and sour cream. Heat, but do not boil. Place chicken in 9x13-inch baking dish; pour sauce over top. Bake at 350° for 60 minutes or until tender. Makes 6 servings.

CHICKEN WITH SOUR CREAM GRAVY

TOP OF STOVE

Serve the gravy over the chicken and mashed potatoes. Add hot buttered peas and rolls and your have a delicious meal without any fuss.

> 1 chicken, cut up
> 3 tablespoons butter or margarine
> Seasoning salt
> 3 tablespoons flour
> 1/4 cup sour cream

Heat butter in large skillet. Brown chicken on both sides. Sprinkle with seasoning salt. Add 1/2 cup water; bring to a boil. Reduce heat and cook, covered, for 20 minutes. Turn chicken; continue cooking 15 to 20 minutes or until tender. Remove chicken and keep warm. In small jar, combine flour and 1/2 cup water; shake to mix well. Gradually add to liquid in skillet; mix well. Cook, stirring constantly, until mixture comes to a boil and thickens. Stir in sour cream, but do not let boil. Taste for seasoning. Makes 4 servings.

GLAZED CHICKEN CURRY

    1 chicken, cut up
    ¹/₄ cup butter
    ¹/₂ cup honey
    ¹/₄ cup Dijon mustard
    1 teaspoon salt
    1 teaspoon curry powder (or to taste)

Heat oven to 350°. Put butter in 9x13-inch baking pan; place in oven to melt. Remove from oven; stir in remaining ingredients. Add chicken, turning to coat. Bake for 60 minutes, basting occasionally with sauce. Chicken should be tender and richly glazed. Makes 4 servings.

BUSY DAY CHICKEN

    4 chicken breast halves, skin removed
    1 cup grated Parmesan cheese
    1 package Uncle Dan's southern-style salad dressing mix
    1 egg, beaten slightly
    ¹/₄ cup butter or margarine, melted

Combine Parmesan cheese and salad dressing mix. Dip chicken in egg, then in cheese mixture. Place on baking sheet. Bake at 425° for 45 minutes or until chicken is golden brown and tender. If chicken appears dry, brush occasionally with melted butter. Makes 4 servings.

CHICKEN DIJON

    4 chicken breast halves
    3 tablespoons butter or margarine
    2 tablespoons flour
    ¹/₂ cup half and half
    1 cup chicken broth
    2 tablespoon Dijon mustard

Melt butter in large heavy skillet. Cook chicken until lightly browned and tender. Remove and keep warm. Add flour to drippings; stir until smooth. Cook about a minute. Add half and half and chicken broth. Cook, stirring frequently, until sauce thickens. Return chicken to skillet, turning to cover with sauce. Cover and cook on low heat about 10 minutes. Makes 4 servings.
TIP: Even though family meals are special, you probably won't take the time to bone the chicken. But for a company dinner, your guests might appreciate not having to work around the bones. Serve with Rice Pilaf, buttered carrots, asparagus spears, and a green salad.

CHICKEN ENCHILADAS   OVEN

    3 whole chicken breasts, cooked
    2 cups sour cream
    1 (4-ounce) can diced green chiles
    3 cans cream of chicken soup
    16 ounces grated Cheddar cheese
    10 (8-inch) flour tortillas

Cut chicken into bite-size pieces. Combine chicken with sour cream, chiles, 1 can soup and 1 cup cheese. Spoon a generous amount of filling down center of each tortilla. Roll up and place, seam-side down, in greased deep 9x13-inch baking pan. Combine remaining 2 cans soup and stir to soften. Spread over tortillas. Sprinkle cheese over top. Bake at 350° for 45 to 60 minutes or until hot and cheese is golden. Makes 8 servings.
TIP: This makes a lot! You may prefer to make just half a recipe. You can also use half Cheddar cheese and half Monterey Jack.

ORANGE GLAZED CHICKEN   OVEN

    1 chicken, cut up
    Salt and pepper
    $1/4$ cup orange juice
    1 tablespoon honey
    $1/4$ teaspoon Worcestershire sauce
    $1/4$ teaspoon dry mustard

Place chicken, skin-side up, in greased shallow baking dish. Sprinkle with salt and pepper. Bake at 350° for 30 minutes. Combine remaining ingredients and brush a little of the sauce over chicken. Continue baking, brushing occasionally with remaining sauce, for 30 minutes. Makes 4 servings.

GOLDEN CHICKEN BAKE   OVEN

    1 chicken, cut up
    Butter
    1 can cream of chicken soup
    1 teaspoon minced dried parsley

Arrange chicken, skin-side down, in shallow baking dish. Place generous dabs of butter over chicken. Bake at 375° for 20 minutes. Turn chicken; bake 20 minutes. Stir soup. Pour over chicken. Sprinkle parsley over top. Bake 20 minutes more. Makes 4 to 6 servings.
TIP: Sauce is very good spooned over the chicken and over rice.

EASY OVEN CHICKEN

> 1 chicken, cut up
> $^1/_2$ cup butter or margarine, melted
> $^3/_4$ teaspoon salt
> $^1/_2$ teaspoon lemon pepper
> $^1/_4$ teaspoon dried basil

Place chicken in 9x13-inch baking dish. Combine remaining ingredients and brush chicken with some of the mixture. Bake at 350° for 60 minutes or until tender, basting frequently with additional butter mixture. Makes 4 servings.

OVEN BAKED HERB CHICKEN

This delicious herbed-flavored chicken is so easy to prepare you will want to make it often. I guarantee your guests will want the recipe.

> 1 chicken, cut up
> 1 (0.7-ounce) package Good Seasons Cheese Garlic salad dressing mix
> 2 tablespoons flour
> $^1/_4$ teaspoon salt
> $^1/_4$ cup butter or margarine, melted
> 1 tablespoon fresh lemon juice

Place chicken, skin-side up, in shallow baking dish. Combine remaining ingredients; brush evenly over top of chicken. Bake at 350° for 60 minutes or until tender and browned. Makes 4 servings.
TIP: Best served hot from the oven. Do not freeze.

MARMALADE CHICKEN

> 1 chicken, cut up
> $^1/_4$ cup butter or margarine, melted
> 1 cup orange marmalade
> $^1/_4$ cup packed light brown sugar
> $^1/_2$ teaspoon dry ginger

Place chicken, skin-side down, in greased 9x13-inch baking dish. Brush with melted butter. Bake at 350° for 15 minutes. Turn chicken, baste with butter, and bake 15 minutes. Combine remaining ingredients and brush on chicken. Bake 30 minutes or until tender and richly glazed, basting frequently. Makes 4 servings.

ORANGE CHICKEN DELIGHT

1 chicken, cut up
1 tablespoon freshly grated orange peel
$1/4$ cup honey
$1/2$ cup oil
2 teaspoons ground ginger

Place chicken, skin-side down, in 9x13-inch baking dish. Combine remaining ingredients; mix well. Baste chicken with some of the mixture. Bake at 350° for 30 minutes, turn and bake 30 minutes, basting frequently. Watch carefully during last 10 minutes of baking time. Makes 4 servings.

LOW-CAL PINEAPPLE CHICKEN

This beats plain poached chicken any day!

4 chicken breast halves
$3/4$ cup unsweetened pineapple juice
$1/4$ cup soy sauce
$1/4$ teaspoon ground ginger
$1/4$ teaspoon freshly ground black pepper

Place chicken, skin-side down, in small baking dish. Combine remaining ingredients and pour $1/4$ cup over top of chicken. Bake at 350° for 60 minutes, basting frequently with the remaining sauce. Makes 4 servings.

OVEN-BARBECUED CHICKEN

$1^1/2$ chickens, cut up
$3/4$ cup honey
1 cup catsup
$1/4$ cup light corn syrup
2 tablespoons Worcestershire sauce
Juice of 1 lemon

Place chicken, skin-side down, in 9x13-inch baking dish. Combine remaining ingredients and pour over top. Marinate at least one hour, basting occasionally. Pour off marinade and reserve. Bake chicken at 350° for 30 minutes. Turn chicken and baste with marinade. Continue baking 30 minutes or until chicken is tender and richly glazed, basting frequently. Makes 6 servings.
TIP: Sauce is delicious served over rice.

PANKO CHICKEN

4 chicken breast halves, skinned, boned
$^1/_2$ cup butter or margarine
1 garlic clove, minced
$^1/_3$ cup Dijon mustard
$1^1/_2$ cups Panko bread crumbs
$^1/_3$ cup grated Parmesan cheese

Heat butter and garlic in small skillet; simmer 5 minutes. Stir in mustard; mix well. Remove from heat and cool slightly. Combine Panko and Parmesan. Dip chicken in butter mixture. Then dip in breading mixture, patting crumbs on to coat well. Cover and chill at least 2 hours to set coating. Bake at 350° for 35 to 45 minutes until golden brown. Makes 4 servings.
TIP: Delicious served with Dijon Mustard Sauce.

PINEAPPLE-ORANGE CHICKEN

1 chicken, cut up
2 (8-ounce) cans crushed pineapple (do not drain)
2 tablespoons butter or margarine, melted
$1^1/_2$ teaspoons ground ginger
1 tablespoon soy sauce

Place chicken, skin-side up, in greased 9x13-inch baking dish. Combine remaining ingredients and spoon over chicken. Bake at 375° for 50 to 60 minutes or until lightly browned. Baste chicken about every 15 minutes. Makes 4 servings.
TIP: If your oven cooks hot, reduce oven temperature to 350° to prevent sauce from burning. Serve with rice, asparagus and Sally Lunn Muffins.

EASY ITALIAN BAKED CHICKEN

1 chicken, cut up
$^1/_2$ cup butter, softened
1 tablespoon garlic salad dressing mix
1 cup Corn Flake crumbs
Paprika

Clean chicken; pat dry with paper towels. Combine butter and salad dressing mix. With spatula or knife, spread mixture over chicken pieces. Roll in crumbs; sprinkle lightly with paprika. Bake at 375° for 60 minutes or until tender. Makes 4 servings.

APPLE-SAUSAGE STUFFING   TOP OF STOVE

Makes enough dressing for one large turkey.

>1 pound seasoned bulk sausage
>1 cup chopped onion
>2 cups chopped apples, peeled
>10 cups seasoned bread cubes for stuffing
>1 egg, slightly beaten
>$^1/_2$ cup chicken broth

In a large skillet, brown sausage. Remove sausage from skillet. Pour off all but 2 tablespoons fat. Add onion and apples to skillet. Cook until onion is tender, about 5 minutes. Combine this mixture with the sausage, bread cubes, egg and broth. Stir until well mixed and bread cubes are coated.
TIP: This recipe has a lot more flavor when cooked in the turkey rather than baked in a casserole.

APRICOT-BREAD STUFFING   TOP OF STOVE

>2 tablespoons butter or margarine
>$^1/_4$ cup finely chopped onion
>$^1/_4$ cup finely chopped dried apricots
>$^1/_3$ cup rich chicken broth
>$^1/_4$ cup finely chopped walnuts
>$1^1/_2$ cups dry bread cubes

Heat butter in small skillet. Add remaining ingredients except bread cubes and cook 3 to 4 minutes or until onion is soft. Pour over bread cubes; toss to coat.
TIP: Makes enough dressing for 1 roasting chicken or 2 Cornish hens.

RICE-NUT STUFFING   TOP OF STOVE

>1 cup uncooked long grain rice
>2 tablespoons butter or margarine
>$^1/_4$ cup finely chopped onion
>$1^1/_4$ cups chicken broth
>$^1/_4$ cup finely chopped pecans
>$^1/_4$ cup flaked coconut

In medium saucepan, sauté rice in butter, stirring often, just until golden. Add onion and broth. Heat to boiling. Reduce heat, cover, and simmer 15 to 20 minutes or until liquid is absorbed and rice is tender. Stir in pecans and coconut.
TIP: Makes enough dressing for 1 roasting chicken or 2 Cornish hens.

Salads, Dressings, & Sauces

ICE COLD SALAD GREENS

A nice cold crisp salad is hard to beat, but sometimes hard to achieve. My favorite method for chilling salad greens works every time, but you do have to allow some chilling time in the refrigerator:

Line a large bowl with several layers of paper towels. Place clean dry greens in bowl. Cover greens with 3 to 4 layers of paper towels. Cover paper towels with one layer of ice cubes. Chill at least 8 hours or overnight. Before serving, if paper towels get too wet, replace with new ones and add additional ice cubes.

QUICK CHEF SALAD

> **For each salad:**
> **Assorted greens, chilled**
> **Chopped fresh mushrooms**
> **Tiny squares thinly sliced ham**
> **Tiny squares thinly sliced cheese**
> **Hard-boiled egg, finely chopped**
> **Choice of dressing**

Place salad greens on an 8-inch salad plate. Top with remaining ingredients in order given and drizzle with dressing.
TIP: Makes a delicious and filling luncheon dish; serve with honey rye bread or rolls.

SPINACH SALAD

> **2 bunches spinach**
> **8 slices bacon, cooked and crumbled**
> **2 hard-boiled eggs, finely chopped**
> **1 can water chestnuts, drained and sliced**
> **1 cup fresh bean sprouts**
> **1 recipe Spinach Salad Dressing (see Index)**

Combine first 5 ingredients in large salad bowl. Pour dressing over to coat lightly; toss and serve. Makes 6 to 8 servings.
TIP: Make dressing ahead and store in refrigerator to use when needed.

ALMOND SPINACH SALAD

1 pound spinach
$^1/_3$ cup sliced or slivered almonds, toasted
6 slices cooked bacon, crumbled
1 small onion, thinly sliced and separated into rings
Vinaigrette dressing

Combine first 4 ingredients in large salad bowl. Toss with enough dressing to lightly coat leaves. Makes 4 to 6 servings.
TIP: For a hearty luncheon dish, add small cubes of Cheddar cheese and ham. Garnish with tomato wedges.

SWEET-SOUR SPINACH SALAD   CHILL

A very popular salad. There is never any left over.

1 bunch fresh spinach
1 very small red onion, thinly sliced, separated into rings
8 slices bacon, cooked, crumbled
1 tablespoon white vinegar
1 tablespoon sugar
$^1/_4$ cup mayonnaise

Wash spinach thoroughly and dry. Remove long stems and tear into bite-size pieces; chill. Combine vinegar, sugar and mayonnaise; chill. When ready to serve combine spinach, onion and bacon. Toss with enough dressing to moisten. Serve immediately — greens have a tendency to get limp if allowed to sit very long. Makes 3 to 4 servings.

CRISP GREEN SALAD

4 cups assorted salad greens
1 cup cherry tomatoes
1 cup cauliflower pieces
$^1/_2$ green pepper, sliced
$^1/_2$ small cucumber, sliced
Choice of dressing

Combine first 5 ingredients in salad bowl. Gently toss with your favorite salad dressing. Makes 6 servings.

HONEY-MUSTARD SALAD   CHILL

¹/₄ cup mild-flavored honey
¹/₄ cup oil
1 tablespoon red wine vinegar
¹/₄ teaspoon dry mustard
¹/₃ cup coarsely chopped walnuts
6 cups assorted greens

Combine first 4 ingredients. Cover and chill. When ready to serve, combine walnuts and salad greens. Drizzle with dressing to coat lightly. Makes 4 servings.

ITALIAN SALAD

Dressing can be made a couple of hours ahead.

1 to 2 heads romaine, torn into bite-size pieces
1 (6-ounce) jar marinated artichoke hearts, drained
³/₄ cup olive oil
¹/₄ cup red wine vinegar
¹/₄ cup grated Parmesan cheese
Salt and pepper to taste

Place romaine in salad bowl. Add artichoke hearts (cut smaller if pieces are too large). Combine remaining ingredients. Toss with just enough dressing to lightly coat leaves. When serving, sprinkle with additional Parmesan cheese, if desired. Makes 4 to 6 servings.

GREEN SALAD WITH SHRIMP

>1 bunch romaine lettuce
>8 ounces small or medium shrimp, cooked
>$1/4$ cup finely chopped green pepper
>1 small onion, thinly sliced and separated
>1 avocado, peeled and thinly sliced
>Choice of dressing

Combine first 5 ingredients in large salad bowl. Add just enough dressing to lightly coat leaves; toss gently and serve. Makes 4 servings.

BROCCOLI-PASTA SALAD   CHILL

>2 cups small shell macaroni, cooked, cooled
>$2^1/2$ cups fresh broccoli, cooked till just tender
>1 cup cherry tomatoes, halved
>$1/2$ cup julienne strips Swiss cheese
>$1/2$ cup Italian dressing

Combine ingredients in large bowl using just enough dressing to coat lightly. Cover and chill. Makes 8 servings.
TIP: For a main course salad, add leftover cooked roast beef, ham or chicken.

STUFFED TOMATOES

>Small to medium-size firm tomatoes
>Desired stuffing
>Lettuce leaves

Remove tops from tomatoes; carefully scoop out seeds and meat; drain. Fill with any one of the following fillings or if using small tomatoes make a double tomato salad using two different fillings:
>Chicken salad garnished with green grapes
>Shrimp salad
>Crab salad
>Tuna salad
>Rice salad garnished with pineapple
>Cooked peas
>Chopped cucumbers with dressing
>Potato salad

SHRIMP STUFFED AVOCADO

    2 avocados
    1¹/₂ cups small cooked shrimp, chilled
    Lettuce leaves
    Mayonnaise or choice of dressing
    Cherry tomatoes

Cut avocados in half lengthwise; discard seed. Fill each half with shrimp; place on lettuce leaves. Top with mayonnaise or choice of dressing. Garnish with tomatoes. Makes 4 servings.

BROCCOLI-TOMATO SALAD

TOP OF STOVE
CHILL

    1 pound fresh broccoli, cut into 1-inch pieces
    1 small tomato, chopped
    ¹/₄ cup finely chopped onion
    ¹/₄ teaspoon salt
    Dash pepper
    ¹/₂ cup mayonnaise

Cook broccoli in small amount of water, until just crisp tender; drain well. Combine broccoli with remaining ingredients, adding just enough mayonnaise to moisten. Cover and chill. Makes 4 servings.

EASY FAMILY COLE SLAW

    4 cups shredded cabbage
    ¹/₂ cup raisins
    ¹/₂ cup mayonnaise
    1 tablespoon milk
    1 tablespoon sugar
    Salt and pepper to taste

Combine cabbage and raisins. In small mixing bowl combine remaining ingredients and pour over cabbage; mix well.

CABBAGE SALAD

CHILL

    3 cups shredded cabbage
    1 medium onion, sliced
    3 tablespoons sugar
    1 teaspoon salt
    2 tablespoons salad oil
    3 tablespoons vinegar

Combine cabbage and onion slices in mixing bowl. Combine remaining ingredients and pour over. Stir to mix. Cover and chill to blend flavors. Makes 4 servings.

MY FAVORITE POTATO SALAD

6 medium red potatoes (about 5 cups diced)
Salt and pepper
2 tablespoons chopped green onion
3 hard-boiled eggs, chopped
$^1/_4$ cup finely chopped celery
$1^1/_4$ cups mayonnaise (approximately)

Cook potatoes in boiling water just until tender. Cool slightly; peel. While still warm, dice potatoes and sprinkle with salt and pepper. Add remaining ingredients; toss gently to mix. Cover and chill several hours or overnight. Makes 8 servings.
TIP: For additional color, add 2 tablespoons finely chopped pimiento. If desired, decorate top of salad with egg slices and tomato wedges; sprinkle with cracked pepper.

TACO SALAD

1 pound lean ground beef
1 ($1^1/_4$-ounce) package Taco seasoning mix
Shredded lettuce
Grated Cheddar cheese
Chopped tomatoes
Salsa (or Thousand Island Dressing)

Brown ground beef; drain. Add seasoning mix and amount of water called for on package. Bring to a boil; reduce heat and simmer uncovered, 15 to 20 minutes, stirring occasionally until liquid is absorbed. Place shredded lettuce in salad bowl; top with ground beef, cheese, tomatoes and sauce. Toss lightly and serve. Makes 4 servings.

CHICKEN SALAD

2 cups cooked finely diced chicken
$^3/_4$ cup finely chopped celery
3 tablespoons finely chopped onion
$^1/_2$ cup chopped slivered almonds
$1^1/_4$ cups mayonnaise (approximately)
Salt and pepper to taste

Combine ingredients in mixing bowl. Cover and chill until ready to use. Makes 4 servings.
TIP: If desired, serve on melon rings or in cantaloupe halves or lettuce cups. Also makes a delicious chicken sandwich or serve on small crackers for a quick snack or appetizer.

CASHEW CHICKEN SALAD   CHILL

 4 cups diced cooked chicken
 $1/3$ cup thinly sliced celery
 $1/3$ cup Angel Flake coconut
 $1/2$ cup grapes, halved
 $1/3$ cup coarsely chopped cashews
 $3/4$ cup mayonnaise

Combine first 5 ingredients. Add mayonnaise to chicken mixture, adding just enough to moisten. Cover and chill. Makes 4 servings.

HAWAIIAN CHICKEN SALAD   CHILL

I have found that men enjoy chicken salad as much as women do. This recipe is a popular one.

 4 cups diced cooked chicken
 $1/2$ cup thinly sliced celery
 $3/4$ cup crushed pineapple, drained
 $1/3$ cup Angel Flake coconut
 $1/4$ teaspoon curry powder (or to taste)
 1 cup mayonnaise

In large mixing bowl, combine first 4 ingredients. Combine curry powder and mayonnaise. Add enough mayonnaise to chicken mixture to coat lightly. Cover and chill. Makes 4 servings.

PINEAPPLE-CASHEW CHICKEN SALAD   CHILL

 4 cups diced cooked chicken
 $3/4$ cup crushed pineapple, drained (save 1 tablespoon juice)
 $1/3$ cup Angel Flake coconut
 $1/3$ cup coarsely chopped cashews
 $3/4$ cup mayonnaise
 Assorted fresh fruit

Combine first 4 ingredients in large mixing bowl. Combine reserved pineapple juice with mayonnaise. Add to chicken mixture, adding just enough to moisten. Cover and chill. Serve with a choice of fruit: Fresh pineapple slices, grape clusters, strawberries, watermelon wedges, cantaloupe balls, Kiwi slices, etc.

TURKEY SALAD   CHILL

>   4 cups leftover cubed turkey
>   1 cup pineapple tidbits, drained
> $1/2$ cup sliced celery
> $1/3$ cup sliced toasted almonds
> $1/2$ cup sour cream
> $1/2$ cup mayonnaise

Place first 4 ingredients in large mixing bowl. Combine sour cream and mayonnaise. Toss with turkey mixture, adding just enough to moisten. Cover and chill. Makes 4 servings.

ARLYS' SHOESTRING SALAD   CHILL

A tasty salad with a delightful crunch.

>   2 cups tuna or diced, cooked chicken
>   1 cup chopped celery
>   1 cup shredded carrots
> $1/3$ cup finely chopped onion
>   1 cup mayonnaise
>   2 cups shoestring potatoes

Combine first 5 ingredients, adding just enough mayonnaise to moisten. Cover and chill. Just before serving, add shoestring potatoes; mix well. Add a little more mayonnaise, if necessary. Makes 4 servings.

PEACHY FRUIT SALAD   TOP OF STOVE
                                                        CHILL

>   1 (6-ounce) package strawberry jello
>   4 cups water
>   1 cup thinly sliced peaches
> $1/2$ cup thinly sliced bananas
> $1/2$ cup thinly sliced strawberries

Heat 2 cups water to boiling. Stir in jello until dissolved. Add remaining 2 cups water. Chill until consistency of unbeaten egg white. Gently fold in fruit. Pour into 6 cup mold; chill until firm. Makes 6 to 8 servings.

CHERRY FREEZE

1 (3-ounce) package cream cheese, softened
1 cup crushed pineapple, drained
2 cups miniature marshmallows
1 cup Royal Ann Cherries, drained, pitted
$^1/_3$ cup quartered Maraschino cherries
1 cup whipping cream, whipped

Combine cream cheese and pineapple; add marshmallows and cherries. Fold in whipped cream. Pour in 10x7-inch dish; freeze. Remove from freezer; cut into squares to serve. Makes 6 to 8 servings.

APPLE JELLO SALAD

1 (3-ounce) package lemon jello
2 cups apple juice
1 cup finely chopped unpared apple (red or green)
1 (2-ounce) package dessert topping mix (Dream Whip)
$^1/_2$ cup cold milk
$^1/_2$ teaspoon vanilla extract

Heat 1 cup of the apple juice to boiling. Add jello and stir to dissolve. Stir in remaining one cup juice. Chill until slightly thickened. Add the chopped apple to one cup of the jello. Pour into 5 cup mold. Chill until almost firm but still sticky to the touch. Prepare topping mix as directed on package, using the cold milk and vanilla; fold in the remaining 1 cup slightly thickened jello. Pour over first layer; chill until set. Makes 6 to 8 servings.
TIP: If desired, add $^1/_4$ cup finely chopped walnuts to first layer. The 5 cup Tupperware jello mold is ideal for this recipe.

PINEAPPLE LIME SALAD

1 (6-ounce) package lime jello
2 cups boiling water
1 (20-ounce) can crushed pineapple (with syrup)
1 cup sour cream, room temperature

Dissolve jello in boiling water. Add crushed pineapple. Chill until slightly thickened. Add sour cream, stirring to blend. Pour into 6 cup ring mold. Chill until set. Makes 8 servings.

MANDARIN FRUIT SALAD CHILL

    2 (11-ounce) cans mandarin oranges, drained
    1 (20-ounce) can pineapple chunks, drained
    1 cup miniature marshmallows
    $1/4$ cup chopped walnuts
    $1/3$ cup mayonnaise
    6 lettuce leaves

Combine first 5 ingredients; toss lightly to coat. Cover and chill until ready to serve. Serve on lettuce leaves.
TIP: To substitute, use whipped cream for the mayonnaise; serve in cantaloupe shells and garnish with fresh strawberries.

FROZEN FRUIT COCKTAIL FREEZE

    2 (3-ounce) packages cream cheese, softened
    1 cup mayonnaise
    1 (30-ounce) can fruit cocktail, well drained
    2 cups miniature marshmallows
    $1/3$ cup Maraschino cherries, quartered
    1 cup whipping cream, whipped

Combine cream cheese and mayonnaise until smooth. Stir in fruit cocktail, marshmallows and cherries. Fold in whipped cream. Pour into buttered shallow 2-quart dish; cover and freeze. Remove from freezer and let stand a few minutes before serving. Makes 12 servings.

EASY STRAWBERRY JELLO SALAD TOP OF STOVE
CHILL

    1 (3-ounce) package strawberry jello
    1 cup boiling water
    1 cup sour cream, room temperature
    1 (10-ounce) package frozen strawberries, thawed

Combine jello and water; stir to dissolve. Stir in sour cream until blended. Add strawberries. Pour into serving dish and chill until set. Makes 6 servings.
TIP: If you have a little difficulty blending in the sour cream, use a rotary beater or mixer at low speed.

PINEAPPLE-STRAWBERRY SALAD

1 cup pineapple chunks
1 pint strawberries
Lettuce leaves
2 tablespoon oil
2 tablespoons lime juice
1 tablespoon honey

Combine pineapple and strawberries; place on lettuce leaves on salad plate. Combine remaining ingredients and drizzle over fruit. Makes 4 servings.

STRAWBERRY NUT SALAD

TOP OF STOVE
CHILL

1 (3-ounce) package strawberry jello
$^1/_2$ cup boiling water
1 (10-ounce) package frozen strawberries, thawed
1 (13-ounce) can crushed pineapple (and juice)
2 medium bananas, mashed
$^1/_2$ cup chopped walnuts

Combine jello and water, stirring to dissolve. Add remaining ingredients. Pour into 5 cup mold. Chill until set. Makes 8 servings.

FROZEN FRUIT SALAD

FREEZE

1 ($3^3/_4$-ounce) package instant vanilla pudding mix
2 cups milk
1 (4-ounce) container Cool Whip, thawed
1 (11-ounce) can mandarin oranges, drained
1 (16-ounce) can fruit cocktail, drained
3 bananas, sliced

Prepare pudding mix with milk as directed on package. Stir in Cool Whip. Add the remaining ingredients. Pour into 7x11-inch dish. Cover and freeze. Remove from freezer 1 hour before serving. Makes 8 to 10 servings.
TIP: Equally as delicious served without freezing.

ORANGE SHERBET SALAD

TOP OF STOVE
CHILL

   1 (6-ounce) package orange jello
   2 cups liquid (part water and part juice)
   1 pint orange sherbet, softened
   2 (11-ounce) cans mandarin oranges, save juice
   1 (8-ounce) can crushed pineapple, save juice
   1 cup whipping cream, whipped

Pour juice in measuring cup; add water to make 2 cups. Heat to boiling in saucepan. Remove from heat; add jello and stir until dissolved. Add sherbet; stir until melted. Chill until just slightly thickened. Add mandarin oranges and pineapple; fold in whipped cream. Pour into a mold or 10x17-inch flat dish. Chill until set. Makes 8 servings.

ALL SEASONS FRUIT BOWL

   6 canned pear halves, chilled
   3 medium bananas, sliced
   2 small apples, cut into cubes
   2 (11-ounce) cans mandarin oranges, chilled
   1 1/2 cups sliced fresh strawberries
   1 (4-ounce) container Cool Whip, thawed

When ready to serve, drain fruit. Slice pears. Combine with remaining ingredients and toss gently to coat fruit. Makes 6 servings.

FLUFFY CHERRY SALAD

CHILL

This recipe can be used as a salad or a dessert. Can also be served frozen in small muffin cups.

   1 (16-ounce) can cherry pie filling
   3/4 cup crushed pineapple, drained
   1 can Eagle Brand sweetened condensed milk
   1 (14-ounce) container Cool Whip, thawed
   1/2 cup coarsely chopped pecans

Combine all ingredients; mix well. Pour into an attractive serving dish and chill until ready to serve. Makes 8 servings.

GREEN FRUIT SALAD   CHILL

One of those recipes you can use as a salad or a light dessert.

> **1 (12-ounce) container Cool Whip, thawed**
> **1 (3-ounce) package pistachio instant pudding mix**
> **1 (11-ounce) can mandarin oranges, save 3 tablespoons juice**
> **1 (17-ounce) can chunky mixed fruits, drained**
> **2 cups miniature marshmallows**

In large bowl, combine Cool Whip and pudding mix with the reserved juice. Gently fold in remaining ingredients. Cover and chill. Makes 6 to 8 servings.

TIP: Fresh fruit can be substituted for the canned fruit.

HONEYDEW SLICES

> **Honeydew melon, chilled, sliced crosswise**
> **Cantaloupe balls**
> **Watermelon balls**
> **Fresh mint leaves (optional)**

Place honeydew slice on individual salad plates. Top each with canta-loupe balls and watermelon balls. Garnish with mint leaves.

TIP: If honeydew melon is too large to make an attractive crosswise slice, you could cut a cantaloupe in crosswise slices and make honey-dew melon balls.

WALDORF SALAD   CHILL

Still a favorite salad with almost everyone.

> **2 Golden Delicious apples, cut into cubes**
> **1 cup sliced celery**
> **$1/3$ cup coarsely chopped walnuts**
> **$1/2$ cup raisins**
> **2 tablespoons lemon juice**
> **$3/4$ cup mayonnaise**

Combine first 5 ingredients. Add mayonnaise and gently toss to coat. Chill until ready to serve. Makes 4 servings.

TIP: For a main course salad add 2 cups cooked cubed chicken.

ALMOST CAESAR SALAD DRESSING

> 3 tablespoons sour cream
> 1 egg, beaten slightly
> 1 teaspoon garlic salt
> $^1/_2$ teaspoon freshly ground black pepper
> 3 tablespoons olive oil
> 2 teaspoons tarragon or white-wine vinegar

Combine ingredients and mix well. (Dressing shouldn't be allowed to stand more than an hour before serving.) Makes about $^1/_3$ cup.
TIP: For a wonderful salad combination, toss with romaine, freshly grated Parmesan cheese, cooked crumbled bacon and croutons.

OLD FASHIONED MUSTARD DRESSING   CHILL

> $^1/_4$ cup mayonnaise
> 2 tablespoons red wine vinegar
> 1 tablespoon Dijon mustard
> 1 teaspoon salt
> $^1/_2$ teaspoon sugar
> 1 cup salad oil

Combine first 5 ingredients in small mixing bowl. Gradually beat in oil until thick and creamy, about 2 minutes. Cover and chill to blend flavors. Makes about $1^1/_2$ cups.

THOUSAND ISLAND DRESSING   CHILL

> $^1/_2$ cup mayonnaise
> $^1/_4$ cup whipping cream, whipped
> 2 tablespoons finely chopped pimiento
> $^1/_4$ cup chopped sweet pickles or pickle relish
> 1 tablespoon finely chopped onion
> $^1/_3$ cup chili sauce

Combine ingredients. Chill to blend flavors.

SOUR CREAM-HONEY DRESSING   CHILL

> 1 cup sour cream
> 3 tablespoons honey
> 3 tablespoons lemon juice
> 1 tablespoon freshly grated lemon peel
> $^1/_4$ teaspoon salt

Combine ingredients until blended. Store in refrigerator to blend flavors. Serve over fruit salads or assorted greens. Makes $1^1/_4$ cups.

TARRAGON SALAD DRESSING

CHILL

$^1/_2$ cup mayonnaise
$^1/_4$ cup sour cream
$1^1/_2$ teaspoons tarragon vinegar
1 tablespoon lemon juice
$^1/_4$ cup finely chopped green onions
$^1/_4$ cup cooked bacon, crumbled

Combine ingredients until blended. Chill several hours to blend flavors. Stir before serving. Makes 1 $^1/_4$ cups.
TIP: This is very good served over a tossed green salad with tomatoes and sliced mushrooms.

SPINACH SALAD DRESSING I

CHILL

1 cup salad oil
$^3/_4$ cup sugar
$^1/_3$ cup catsup
$^1/_4$ cup white vinegar
$^1/_4$ cup finely chopped onion
2 teaspoons Worcestershire sauce

Place ingredients in blender or food processor; blend until smooth. Cover and chill. Serve over spinach or Spinach Salad (see Index). Makes about 2 $^1/_2$ cups.

SPINACH SALAD DRESSING II

TOP OF STOVE

2 tablespoons bacon drippings
$^1/_4$ cup cider vinegar
1 tablespoon sugar
$^1/_2$ teaspoon salt
$^1/_4$ teaspoon dry mustard
$^1/_4$ teaspoon pepper

Combine ingredients and add 2 tablespoons water. Pour into small saucepan; cook until mixture comes to a boil, stirring to dissolve sugar. Pour over spinach or other salad greens to lightly coat leaves. Serve right away. Makes about $^1/_2$ cup.
TIP: A delicious addition to the greens would be crumbled cooked bacon, sliced green onions, and sliced raw mushrooms.

DIETER'S SALAD DRESSING   CHILL

$1/2$ teaspoon dry mustard
$1/2$ teaspoon salt
$1/4$ teaspoon pepper
6 packets sugar substitute
$1/4$ cup red wine vinegar
$1/4$ cup fresh lemon juice

Combine ingredients in small jar; chill. Makes about $1/2$ cup.
TIP: For additional flavor, add 2 tablespoons finely chopped onion.

BASIC FRENCH DRESSING   CHILL

$3/4$ cup oil
$1/4$ cup red wine vinegar
$1/2$ teaspoon sugar
1 teaspoon seasoned salt
$1/4$ teaspoon pepper
$1/2$ teaspoon paprika

Combine ingredients in jar. Chill to blend flavors. Makes 1 cup.
TIP: Adding $1/4$ teaspoon dry mustard will prevent dressing from separating so quickly.

FRENCH DRESSING   CHILL

$1/2$ cup oil
$1/2$ cup white vinegar
$1/2$ cup catsup
$1/2$ cup sugar
1 teaspoon seasoning salt

Combine ingredients; mix well. Chill at least an hour to blend flavors. Makes $1^1/2$ cups.

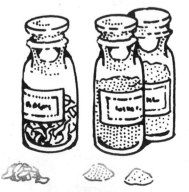

ROQUEFORT DRESSING

TOP OF STOVE

8 ounces Roquefort cheese
1 (13-ounce) can evaporated milk
1 quart mayonnaise
2 small garlic cloves, minced

Combine Roquefort and milk in top of double boiler. Cook over low heat until cheese is melted, stirring until blended and smooth. Add mayonnaise and garlic. Cover and chill overnight to blend flavors. Makes about 1 quart.
TIP: This is a large recipe, but will keep several weeks in refrigerator. May also be used as a dip with fresh vegetables or chips.

QUICK ROQUEFORT DRESSING

1 jar Aunt Marie's Roquefort Dressing
Sour cream

Mix together equal parts of dressing and sour cream. Cover and chill until ready to use.
TIP: Aunt Marie's Roquefort Dressing can be purchased in the produce department of most grocery stores.

CREAMY ITALIAN DRESSING

CHILL

$^{3}/_{4}$ cup sour cream
$^{1}/_{3}$ cup mayonnaise
$^{1}/_{4}$ cup milk
1 (0.6-ounce) package Italian dressing mix
2 tablespoons sugar
$^{1}/_{8}$ teaspoon salt

Combine ingredients until well mixed. Chill to blend flavors. Serve over lettuce wedges or a tossed green salad. Makes about $1^{1}/_{4}$ cups.
TIP: You can also serve as a dip with assorted fresh vegetables or crackers. For variety, add chopped tomato, diced cucumber and sliced mushrooms and serve over lettuce.

ITALIAN DRESSING

    1 cup oil
    6 tablespoons red wine vinegar
    2 small cloves garlic, minced
    1 teaspoon salt
    $1/4$ teaspoon pepper
    $1/2$ teaspoon dry mustard

Combine ingredients in jar; shake well. You can use right away or chill until ready to serve. Makes $1^1/4$ cups.
TIP: If desired, add $1/2$ teaspoon oregano and/or other herbs.

VINAIGRETTE DRESSING   CHILL

    $1/2$ cup white vinegar
    $1^1/2$ teaspoons salt
    $1/4$ teaspoon pepper
    $1/2$ teaspoon dry mustard
    1 garlic clove, minced
    1 cup salad oil

Combine first 5 ingredients and blend. Add oil and stir until blended. Store in tightly covered jar in refrigerator. Will keep for several weeks. Makes $1^1/2$ cups.
TIP: One teaspoon sugar added to above mixture improves the flavor for some, but you may prefer to omit.

VINAIGRETTE-DIJON DRESSING

1^1/$_2$ teaspoons Dijon mustard
^{1}/$_2$ teaspoon sugar
^{1}/$_4$ teaspoon salt
^{1}/$_4$ teaspoon pepper
2 tablespoons red wine vinegar
^{1}/$_4$ cup olive oil

Combine first 5 ingredients. Beating with a wire whisk, slowly dribble in oil until mixture thickens and ingredients are thoroughly blended. Makes about ^{1}/$_3$ cup.
TIP: Dressing is best made just before serving.

WALNUT OIL DRESSING   CHILL

7 tablespoons walnut oil
3 tablespoons red wine vinegar
2 tablespoons Dijon mustard
^{1}/$_4$ teaspoon minced dried parsley
^{1}/$_4$ teaspoon salt
^{1}/$_8$ teaspoon pepper

Combine ingredients and, using a whisk, beat until smooth. Chill. Makes ^{2}/$_3$ cup.
TIP: Walnut oil is expensive and sometimes hard to find. You can still get a walnut flavor by using regular salad oil and adding walnuts to the salad.

SWEET-SOUR DRESSING   CHILL

^{3}/$_4$ cup mayonnaise
3 tablespoons sugar
3 tablespoon white vinegar
^{1}/$_4$ teaspoon salt
^{1}/$_8$ teaspoon pepper
^{1}/$_2$ teaspon parsley

Combine ingredients and mix well. Cover and chill at least 2 hours to blend flavors. Makes 1 cup.
TIP: I like to add this to a whole-meal salad of shredded lettuce, cubed chicken, crumbled cooked bacon, and slivered almonds. Very good!

CREAMY LEMON-DILL DRESSING

    1 cup sour cream
    2 tablespoons fresh lemon juice
    2 teaspoons sugar
    $1/2$ teaspoon dill weed
    Dash pepper

Combine ingredients; mix well. Serve on assorted salad greens or hot buttered asparagus or broccoli. Makes 1 cup.

DIJON MUSTARD DRESSING   CHILL

A dressing that will keep about a month in the refrigerator.

    1 tablespoon Dijon mustard
    1 small garlic clove, minced
    $1/8$ teaspoon freshly ground pepper
    1 egg yolk
    2 tablespoons red wine vinegar
    $1/2$ cup oil

In small mixer bowl, combine mustard, garlic and pepper. Beat in egg yolk and vinegar; mix well. Add oil, about 1 teaspoon at a time, till half the oil has been added. Add remaining oil in a thin steady stream. Chill. Makes about $1/2$ cup.

COMPANY CHAMPAGNE DRESSING   CHILL

    $1/4$ cup champagne vinegar
    $1^1/2$ teaspoons Dijon mustard
    2 egg yolks
    $1/2$ teaspoon salt
    $1/8$ teaspoon pepper
    1 cup oil

In blender or food processor, combine first 5 ingredients. Process for about a minute. With motor running, add oil in a slow steady stream. Dressing should be well mixed and creamy. Chill. Makes about $1^3/4$ cups.

POPPY SEED DRESSING

Use as a dressing for your favorite spinach salad or drizzle over a fresh fruit salad. Will keep several days in the refrigerator.

> $^1/_2$ **cup salad oil**
> **3 tablespoons cider vinegar**
> **6 tablespoons sugar**
> $^1/_2$ **teaspoon salt**
> $^1/_2$ **teaspoon dry mustard**
> **1 tablespoon poppy seeds**

In mixer bowl, at low speed, combine the first 5 ingredients. Beat until well mixed and mixture has thickened. Stir in poppy seeds. Chill at least 2 hour to blend flavors. Makes about 1 cup.

CHOCOLATE SAUCE

TOP OF STOVE

$^1/_2$ cup butter
4 (1-ounce) squares unsweetened chocolate
3 cups sugar
1 teaspoon vanilla extract
1 (13-ounce) can evaporated milk

Melt butter in top of double boiler. Add chocolate squares; heat until melted, stirring to blend. Add sugar, $^1/_4$ cup at a time, stirring until sugar is moistened (it will become quite thick and dry at this point). Stir in vanilla. Add milk a little at a time, stirring to mix well. Pour into jar and store in refrigerator; sauce will thicken as it sets. Serve hot or cold. Makes 4 cups.

CHOCOLATE CRACKLE SAUCE

TOP OF STOVE

Kids love this.

$^1/_4$ cup butter or margarine
1 (6-ounce) package semi-sweet chocolate chips
1 cup finely chopped walnuts (optional)

In heavy saucepan, melt butter and chocolate chips. Stir until smooth. If using walnuts, add to chocolate mixture. Pour over ice cream. Sauce will become firm and chewy. Makes $1^1/_2$ cups.

PEANUT BUTTER-CHOCOLATE SAUCE

TOP OF STOVE

$^2/_3$ cup sugar
2 tablespoons light corn syrup
1 cup water
2 (1-ounce) squares semi-sweet chocolate
$^1/_2$ teaspoon vanilla extract
$^1/_2$ cup creamy peanut butter

In small heavy saucepan, combine first 4 ingredients. Bring to a full boil, stirring frequently. Reduce heat and simmer 3 to 4 minutes. Mixture should be smooth and slightly thickened. Remove from heat; stir in vanilla and peanut butter. Makes $1^1/_2$ cups.
TIP: Serve hot over ice cream or drizzle sauce over some desserts.

WHOLE BERRY CRANBERRY SAUCE

1 pound fresh whole cranberries
2 cups sugar
³/₄ cup cold water
¹/₂ cup apricot jam or preserves
¹/₄ cup fresh lemon juice

Wash cranberries, remove the bad ones. In large saucepan, combine sugar and water. Bring to a boil and cook 3 to 4 minutes. Add cranberries and cook 6 to 8 minutes. Cranberries will burst; cause a popping sound and become transparent. Remove from heat and stir in apricot jam and lemon juice. Cover and chill before serving. Mixture will be a little thin but will thicken as it chills. Makes about 4 cups.
TIP: Serve with turkey dinner or hot turkey sandwiches.

CHUNKY APPLESAUCE

You'll never want to buy applesauce again.

5 large Golden Delicious apples
5 large Rome apples
³/₄ cup sugar
¹/₂ teaspoon cinnamon
Dash ginger
5 large strips orange peel

Peel, core and slice apples into ¹/₄ to ¹/₂-inch slices. You should have about 12 cups. Put apples and remaining ingredients in large heavy pan. Pour ¹/₂ cup water over top. Cover; simmer 45 to 60 minutes or until apples are just tender. Don't let apples get too soft. Remove from heat and discard orange peel. Let cool. Store in refrigerator. Makes about 5 cups.

ORANGE-RAISIN SAUCE

Very good served over ham or pork.

²/₃ cup orange juice
1 cup water
2 tablespoons cornstarch
¹/₈ teaspoon ground allspice
¹/₂ cup orange marmalade
1 cup raisins

In small saucepan, combine first 4 ingredients. Heat, stirring constantly, until mixture thickens. Stir in marmalade and raisins. Heat through. Makes 2 cups.

MUSTARD SAUCE   CHILL

1 cup whipping cream, whipped
$1/2$ cup mayonnaise
$1/4$ cup prepared mustard

Combine ingredients until blended. Cover and chill at least 2 to 3 hours
to blend flavors. Makes about 1 $1/4$ cups. *
TIP: Serve with ham.

DIJON MUSTARD SAUCE   CHILL

$1/4$ cup Dijon mustard
$1/4$ cup mayonnaise

Combine ingredients and mix to blend. Cover and chill until ready to
serve. Makes $1/2$ cup.
TIP: Serve with Panko Chicken or Chicken Nuggets.

CREAM FRAICHE   CHILL

1 cup heavy cream
1 cup sour cream

Combine heavy cream and sour cream in small bowl. Cover loosely
with plastic wrap and let stand, at room temperature, overnight or until
thickened. Bowl should be placed in a warm area of the kitchen. Cover
and refrigerate until well-chilled before serving. Makes 2 cups.
TIP: Cream Fraiche is good served over fresh fruit, especially strawberries, and over fruit desserts and molded salads. In some recipes, it can
also be substituted for sour cream.

MAYONNAISE   CHILL

Mayonnaise is so easy to make, I'm surprised we don't make it more often.

2 tablespoons lemon juice or vinegar
$1/2$ teaspoon salt
1 teaspoon dry mustard
1 egg
1 cup oil, separated

In blender, place first 4 ingredients along with $1/4$ cup oil. Turn blender
on, remove cover and slowly add remaining oil. Cover and store in
refrigerator. Makes $1^1/4$ cups.
VARIATION: Add your choice of pepper, Dijon mustard, garlic powder, basil, etc.

MOCK HOLLANDAISE SAUCE   TOP OF STOVE

So easy.

   $^1/_2$ **cup sour cream**
   $^1/_2$ **cup mayonnaise**
   2 teaspoons fresh lemon juice
   1 teaspoon prepared mustard

In small saucepan, combine all the ingredients and cook over very low
heat until heated through. Makes 1 cup.
TIP: Serve warm over cooked asparagus, broccoli, or green beans. Can
be made ahead and reheated.

CLARIFIED BUTTER   TOP OF STOVE

   1 pound butter

Melt butter in small saucepan. Pour melted butter into glass measuring
cup; let stand. Skim off foam. Carefully pour off butter and discard the
milky sediment that accumulates on the bottom. Refrigerate and use as
needed. Makes about $1^1/_2$ cups.
TIP: Clarified butter will not burn as easily as plain butter. Use to sauté
fish, chicken, chops, French toast, etc.

ORANGE-HONEY BUTTER

   $^1/_2$ **cup butter**
   $^1/_4$ **cup honey**
   2 teaspoons freshly grated orange peel

Whip butter until fluffy. Gradually add honey and orange peel; mix
until blended. Makes about $^3/_4$ cup.
TIP: To substitute, use fresh lemon peel for the orange peel. Serve on
breads and French toast. Cover and store leftover butter in the refrigerator.

ORANGE CREAM CHEESE   CHILL

Serve with sweet-type crackers, or on muffins, French toast and pancakes.

   1 (8-ounce) package cream cheese, softened
   $^3/_4$ **cup sifted powdered sugar**
   1 tablespoon frozen orange juice concentrate
   1 tablespoon grated orange peel
   1 tablespoon Grand Marnier Liqueur

Cream the cheese until smooth. Add remaining ingredients and mix
until blended and smooth. Cover and chill. Makes $1^1/_4$ cups.

CHEDDAR CHEESE SPREAD

Great on French bread.

> 1 cup (4-ounces) grated Cheddar cheese
> $^1/_2$ cup mayonnaise
> 2$^1/_2$ tablespoons finely minced onion
> French bread, sliced
> Grated Parmesan cheese

Combine ingredients and mix well. Put in small buttered baking dish. Bake at 400° for 20 minutes or until heated through. Spread on bread slices. Sprinkle with Parmesan. Broil until bubbly and light golden brown.
TIP: Very good servd with salad or soup. Serve with small bread slices for appetizers.

MAPLE FLAVORED SYRUP

> $^1/_2$ cup firmly packed light brown sugar
> 1 cup light corn syrup
> $^1/_2$ cup water
> 1 tablespoon butter
> $^1/_4$ teaspoon maple flavoring (Mapleine)

Combine ingredients in small saucepan. Cook over low heat to dissolve sugar; simmer 5 minutes. Serve right away or cool and store in refrigerator until ready to use. Makes 1$^3/_4$ cups.
TIP: Flavor improves if allowed to stand overnight.

EASY BORDELAISE SAUCE

> 4 tablespoons minced shallots (or onion)
> 4 tablespoons butter
> 2 bay leaves, finely crumbled
> 1 cup red Burgundy wine
> 5 teaspoons cornstarch
> 1$^1/_2$ cups canned beef broth or bouillon (undiluted)

In saucepan, sauté shallots in 2 tablespoons of the butter until tender but not browned. Add crumbled bay leaves and wine; simmer over medium heat until reduced to about one-third its original volume. Combine cornstarch and about $^1/_4$ cup beef broth, mixing to form a smooth paste. Stir into wine mixture along with remaining beef broth. Cook, stirring frequently, until sauce thickens. Add remaining 2 tablespoons butter. Makes about 2 cups.
TIP: Excellent served with steaks or beef fondue.

WHITE SAUCE

Sauce	Butter	Flour	Salt	Pepper	Milk
Thin	2 tbsp.	2 tbsp.	1 tsp.	$1/4$ tsp.	2 cups
Medium	4 tbsp.	4 tbsp.	1 tsp.	$1/4$ tsp.	2 cups
Thick	8 tbsp.	8 tbsp.	1 tsp.	$1/4$ tsp.	2 cups

Melt butter in heavy saucepan over low heat; stir in flour, salt and pepper, stirring until well blended. Remove from heat. Add milk all at once; stir until blended. Return to heat; cook, stirring constantly, until thickened and smooth. Makes 2 cups.
TIP: For 1 cup sauce, make half the recipe.

CHEESE SAUCE

3 tablespoons butter
3 tablespoons flour
1 cup milk or half and half
$1/2$ cup (2-ounces) grated Cheddar cheese
$1/2$ cup (2-ounces) grated American cheese
1-2 tablespoons sherry

Melt butter in saucepan; stir in flour and cook a couple of minutes, but do not allow to brown. Remove from heat and add milk all at once. Stir until blended and smooth; cook over low heat, stirring constantly, until thickened. Add cheese and sherry, stir until cheese is melted and sauce is hot, but do not boil. Makes $1^1/2$-2 cups.
TIP: This sauce is absolutely delicious served over baked potatoes. Pass the sauce and let everyone pour their own.

SNAPPY HORSERADISH SAUCE

$1/2$ cup sour cream
$1/4$ cup mayonnaise
$1^1/2$ teaspoons prepared horseradish
$1/4$ teaspoon onion salt
$1/4$ teaspoon garlic salt

Combine ingredients and mix thoroughly. Cover and chill at least 1 hour to blend flavors. Makes $3/4$ cup.
TIP: For that special dinner, fill large mushroom caps with sauce; garnish with finely chopped chives or green onions and bake at 325° for 10 to 15 minutes. Serve on dinner plate with prime rib, roast beef, etc.

QUICK CHEESE SAUCE   TOP OF STOVE

   1 cup canned evaporated milk
   2 cups processed American cheese, diced
   $1/4$ teaspoon dry mustard
   $1/2$ teaspoon Worcestershire sauce
   Dash paprika

Heat milk in saucepan over low heat. Add cheese and cook, stirring constantly, until melted. Stir in remaining ingredients. Serve hot. Makes 2 cups.
TIP: Use as a hot sauce for baked potatoes, vegetables, etc.

TARTAR SAUCE   CHILL

   $3/4$ cup mayonnaise
   1 teaspoon finely chopped or grated onion
   1 tablespoon finely chopped fresh parsley
   1 tablespoon finely chopped sweet pickle
   1 tablespoon finely chopped green olives

Combine ingredients in small mixing bowl. Cover; refrigerate at least 1 hour to blend flavors. Makes 1 cup.

PIZZA SAUCE

   $1/4$ teaspoon garlic powder
   $1/4$ teaspoon oregano
   $1/2$ teaspoon basil
   $1/2$ cup grated Parmesan cheese
   1 (8-ounce) can tomato sauce

In small mixing bowl, combine all the ingredients and mix well. Makes about 1 cup.

BARBECUE SAUCE   TOP OF STOVE

A quick barbecue sauce for chicken, hamburgers, pork and spareribs.

   1 (8-ounce) can tomato sauce
   $1/3$ cup white vinegar
   $1/3$ cup packed light brown sugar
   $1/3$ cup finely chopped onion
   2 tablespoons prepared mustard
   1 tablespoon chili powder

In small saucepan, combine all the ingredients and bring to a boil. Reduce heat and simmer 5 minutes. Makes 2 cups.
TIP: Can make ahead and refrigerate. Will keep about one week.

DELUXE BARBECUE SAUCE

> 1 cup bottled barbecue sauce
> $^3/_4$ cup catsup
> 2 tablespoons light brown sugar
> 2 tablespoons lemon juice
> 2 tablespoons Worcestershire sauce
> 1 tablespoon prepared horseradish

Combine ingredients in saucepan; heat through. Makes 2 cups.
TIP: For a different taste treat, use Kraft's Sweet and Sour Sauce and omit the brown sugar.

STIR-FRY SAUCE

This is a very good sauce for almost any combination of stir-fry.

> 1 teaspoon cornstarch
> $^3/_4$ teaspoon sugar
> $1^1/_2$ teaspoons wine vinegar
> 2 teaspoons water
> $2^1/_2$ tablespoons soy sauce
> Dash Tabasco

Combine ingredients mixing well to blend. Use as the sauce for stir-fry such as: beef, pork, chicken, vegetables, etc.

SWEET AND SOUR SAUCE

Serve with Chicken Nuggets, Chicken Wings, Egg Rolls, etc.

> $^1/_4$ cup cold water
> 4 teaspoons cornstarch
> $^1/_3$ cup peach-pineapple preserves or pineapple preserves
> $^1/_3$ cup packed light brown sugar
> $^1/_3$ cup white vinegar
> 2 tablespoons catsup

In small saucepan, combine water and cornstarch, until smooth. Add remaining ingredients. Cook, stirring constantly until mixture thickens. Cool. Makes $1^1/_4$ cups.

CHINESE BEEF MARINADE

    1 teaspoon cornstarch
    2 teaspoons soy sauce
    1 teaspoon sugar
    1 pound Flank or round steak

Combine cornstarch and soy sauce, mixing until smooth. Stir in sugar. Cut meat crossgrain into long narrow strips; put in small bowl. Sprinkle marinade over meat; toss to mix. Let stand 2 to 3 hours or longer, if desired, (even overnight, in which case you would cover and refrigerate). Use meat in favorite Chinese (or other) recipes.
TIP: A great meat tenderizer.

EASY STEAK MARINADE

    $^1/_4$ cup soy sauce
    $^1/_4$ cup salad oil
    2 tablespoons fresh lemon juice
    1 tablespoon light brown sugar
    $^1/_4$ teaspoon garlic salt
    $^1/_8$ teaspoon oregano

Combine ingredients in small mixing bowl, stirring to blend. Use to marinate steaks such as sirloin and chuck (or any other kind). Marinate several hours, turning occasionally.

TERIYAKI MARINADE I

    $^1/_3$ cup soy sauce
    $^1/_2$ cup oil
    1 tablespoon lemon juice
    2 tablespoons sherry
    1 teaspoon ground ginger
    1 garlic clove, minced

Combine ingredients and mix well (oil will tend to separate). Pour over beef, ribs, pork, chicken or fish. Marinate several hours or overnight. Brush food with marinade while cooking. Makes 1 cup.
TIP: Marinades with sugar have a tendency to burn and should be used for basting toward the end of the cooking time. This recipe can be used throughout the cooking time and will prevent food from getting too dry.

TERIYAKI MARINADE II

1 cup soy sauce
1 cup dry sherry
$^1/_4$ cup sugar
2 cloves garlic
1 teaspoon ground ginger

Combine ingredients in jar; shake to mix well. Store in refrigerator if not using right away. Makes 2 cups.
TIP: Use as a marinade for any kind of shish kabob and for beef, chicken and pork. Brush with marinade the last few minutes of cooking time.

ROAST PAN GRAVY   TOP OF STOVE

$^1/_4$ cup fat from roast
$^1/_4$ cup flour
2 cups liquid (meat juices plus water or broth)
Salt and pepper

Remove roast and keep warm. Pour meat juices and fat into large measuring cup, leaving crusty bits in pan. Skim off fat, reserving 4 tablespoons. Return fat to pan and heat until bubbly. Stir in flour. Blend until smooth. Cook over low heat, stirring frequently, until mixture is thickened. Remove pan from heat. Add 2 cups liquid all at once; stir to mix well. Return to heat and bring to a boil. Reduce heat and simmer 3 to 4 minutes. Add salt and pepper to taste. Makes 2 cups.

CREAM GRAVY   TOP OF STOVE

4 tablespoons fat, from frying chicken (or other meats)
4 tablespoons flour
2 cups milk
Salt and pepper

Leave 4 tablespoons fat in pan along with the crusty bits that stick to the bottom. Heat until hot. Stir in flour until blended. Cook until brown and bubbly, stirring constantly. Add milk; stir to mix well. Continue cooking, stirring frequently, until gravy is thickened, about 5 minutes. Add salt and pepper to taste. Makes 2 cups.
TIP: If gravy is too thick, stir in a little milk. If too thin, add a little flour mixed with a small amount of water.

TURKEY GRAVY   TOP OF STOVE

$^1/_2$ **cup fat drippings**
$^1/_2$ **cup flour**
4 cups turkey stock (from turkey or from cooking giblets)
Salt and pepper

When turkey is done, pour meat juices into large measuring cup. Fat will rise to the top. Pour off $^1/_2$ cup fat and pour into medium saucepan. Discard remaining fat, leaving the turkey stock. Set saucepan on burner; reheat the fat. Stir in flour; cook over low heat until lightly browned. Add 4 cups turkey stock, stirring constantly to blend. Cook over medium heat, stirring frequently, until thickened and smooth. Season with salt and pepper. Makes 4 cups.
TIP: If you don't have 4 cups turkey stock, add water to make up the difference. If too thin, stir in additional flour mixed with a small amount of water or stock. Add diced cooked turkey to leftover gravy. Reheat and serve over mashed potatoes, rice or noodles.

BROWN GRAVY   TOP OF STOVE

Use this recipe to make gravy to serve with leftovers. For each cup of gravy desired, you will need:

2 tablespoons butter
$^1/_2$ **teaspoon sugar (for browning)**
2 tablespoons flour
1 cup hot water
1 beef bouillon cube, crumbled
Salt and pepper

Melt butter in saucepan over low heat. Add sugar; cook 2 minutes, stirring occasionally. Add flour; cook about 3 minutes or until flour is lightly browned. Stir in water and bouillon cube, stirring until smooth. Add salt and pepper to taste. Cook over low heat 5 minutes to blend flavors. Makes 1 cup.
TIP: Additional seasonings such as minced onion, garlic powder, celery salt, etc. can be added. If a darker gravy is desired, stir in a few drops of Kitchen Bouquet.

Vegetables

STIR-FRY ASPARAGUS   TOP OF STOVE

    1 pound fresh asparagus
    2 tablespoons oil
    $1/8$-inch slice fresh ginger, size of a quarter
    2 teaspoons soy sauce
    $1/4$ cup chicken broth or bouillon
    $1/2$ teaspoon cornstarch

Wash asparagus. Snap off bottom end of asparagus where it breaks easily. Cut diagonally into 1-inch pieces. Place in rapidly boiling water; remove from heat and let stand 4 minutes. Drain. Add oil to large skillet or wok; heat until very hot. Add ginger and stir about 1 minute; remove ginger. Add asparagus and cook until heated through. Combine soy sauce, chicken broth and cornstarch in small dish; stir until smooth. Add to asparagus. Simmer 2 to 3 minutes. Asparagus should be crisp tender. Makes 3 to 4 servings.
TIP: Fresh broccoli may be substituted for asparagus. If desired, add sliced water chestnuts.

ASPARAGUS CASSEROLE   OVEN

    2 cups saltine cracker crumbs
    $1/2$ cup melted butter or margarine
    2 cups (8-ounces) grated Cheddar cheese, divided
    1 (16-ounce) can asparagus, save juice
    1 can cream of mushroom soup
    $1/2$ cup slivered almonds or chopped pecans

Combine cracker crumbs, butter and $1 1/2$ cups of the cheese. Measure out $1/2$ cup of mixture and reserve for top. Put remaining mixture in greased $1 1/2$-quart deep casserole, using half the asparagus, soup mixture, cheese and nuts. Repeat. Sprinkle reserved cracker mixture over top. Bake at 350° for 20 minutes or until heated through. Makes 6 servings.

EASY BAKED BEANS   OVEN

    2 (16-ounce) cans pork and beans
    $1/2$ cup firmly packed light brown sugar
    1 teaspoon dry mustard
    $1/2$ cup catsup
    6 slices bacon, diced

Combine pork and beans, brown sugar, mustard and catsup. Pour into greased $1 1/2$-quart casserole. Top with diced bacon. Bake at 325° for 2 to $2 1/2$ hours. Makes 6 servings.
TIP: An addition of $1/2$ cup drained crushed pineapple is very good.

DEVILED GREEN BEANS

TOP OF STOVE

1 (16-ounce) can green beans, drained
1 medium onion, thinly sliced
3 tablespoons butter
1 tablespoon prepared horseradish
1 tablespoon prepared mustard

Sauté onion in butter until golden. Add horseradish, mustard and then green beans; mix well. Cook until heated through. Makes 4 servings.

GREEN BEANS SUPREME

TOP OF STOVE

1 (16-ounce) can green beans, drained
$1/3$ cup thinly sliced celery
$1/4$ cup slivered almonds
2 tablespoons butter or margarine
Salt and pepper

In medium skillet, sauté celery and almonds in butter until celery is tender and almonds are toasted. Add beans and heat though. Add salt and pepper to taste. Makes 4 servings.
TIP: Sliced mushrooms or water chestnuts make a nice addition.

GERMAN GREEN BEANS

TOP OF STOVE

4 slices bacon
1 tablespoon finely chopped onion
2 tablespoons red wine vinegar
1 tablespoon sugar
1 (16-ounce) can green beans, drained

In small skillet, cook bacon until crisp. Drain, leaving 1 tablespoon of drippings in pan. Add onion and cook until tender. Stir in vinegar and sugar. Crumble bacon and add along with the green beans. Cook until heated through. Makes 3 to 4 servings.

GREEN BEANS DIJON

TOP OF STOVE

1 tablespoon butter or margarine
1 tablespoon chopped almonds
$1^1/2$ teaspoons lemon juice
1 teaspoon Dijon mustard
1 (16-ounce) can green beans, heated, drained

Heat butter in small skillet. Add almonds and toast lightly. Stir in lemon juice and mustard. Pour mixture over hot beans and toss gently to coat. Makes 4 servings.

COMPANY GREEN BEANS OVEN

3 (16-ounce) cans French style green beans, drained
1 (16-ounce) can bean sprouts, drained
1 (8-ounce) can sliced water chestnuts, drained
1 can cream of mushroom soup
1 small onion, finely chopped
1 cup (4-ounces) grated Cheddar cheese

Combine first 5 ingredients in greased 3-quart casserole. Add $^2/_3$ cup of the cheese. Sprinkle remaining cheese on top. Bake at 350° for 30 to 40 minutes. Makes 12 servings.
TIP: Casserole can be mixed ahead to bake later. To substitute, use French fried onion rings for the cheese; add a 4 ounce can sliced mushrooms.

BROCCOLI BAKE OVEN

$^3/_4$ pound fresh broccoli
$^1/_2$ can cream of chicken soup
2 tablespoons milk
$^1/_2$ cup (2-ounces) grated Cheddar cheese
$^1/_2$ cup Bisquick mix
2 tablespoons butter

Place broccoli in ungreased 1-quart round casserole. Combine soup and milk; stir until blended. Pour over broccoli. Sprinkle with cheese. Mix Bisquick and butter until crumbly; sprinkle over cheese. Bake at 400° for 20 minutes or until lightly browned. Makes 6 servings.

BROCCOLI SUPREME OVEN

1 (10-ounce) package frozen chopped broccoli, cooked
1 cup mayonnaise
1 can cream of mushroom soup
6 eggs, beaten lightly
1 cup (4-ounces) grated Cheddar cheese

Let broccoli cool slightly; combine with mayonnaise. Add soup, eggs and $^1/_2$ cup of the grated cheese. Pour into greased $1^1/_2$-quart casserole. Sprinkle remaining cheese on top. Place dish in a larger pan. Fill pan with 1 inch of water. Bake at 350° for 50 to 60 minutes or until set. Makes 8 servings.
TIP: If using a deep casserole dish, it may be necessary to increase baking time.

BROCCOLI WITH SOUR CREAM SAUCE

TOP OF STOVE

1 pound fresh broccoli
$^1/_3$ cup mayonnaise
$^1/_3$ cup sour cream
1 teaspoon prepared mustard
$^1/_2$ teaspoon lemon juice

Cook broccoli until tender; drain. Combine remaining ingredients in small saucepan. Cook over low heat, stirring constantly, until hot but not boiling. Place broccoli in serving dish; pour hot sauce over top. Makes 3 to 4 servings.
TIP: If desired, sprinkle $^1/_4$ cup slivered almonds over top.

BROCCOLI PARMESAN

TOP OF STOVE
OVEN

1 pound cut broccoli, flowers and stems
1 large tomato, sliced
$^2/_3$ cup mayonnaise
$^1/_4$ cup grated Parmesan cheese, divided

Cook broccoli about 2 minutes. Arrange in 8-inch baking dish. Top with tomato slices. Combine mayonnaise and 3 tablespoons Parmesan. Spread over tomato slices. Sprinkle with remaining Parmesan. Bake at 350° for 40 minutes or until heated through and lightly browned. Makes 4 servings.

BROCCOLI STIR-FRY

TOP OF STOVE

4 cups cut broccoli, flowers and stems
1 tablespoon oil
6 thin slices fresh ginger
1 garlic clove, minced
1 teaspoon sugar
$^1/_2$ teaspoon salt

Steam broccoli until tender. Heat oil in large skillet or wok. Add ginger and garlic. Cook, stirring frequently, about a minute. Add broccoli, sugar, salt and one tablespoon water. Cook, stirring frequently, until heated through. Makes 4 servings.
TIP: During the Christmas holidays, add one tablespoon chopped pimiento.

CAULIFLOWER-BROCCOLI DISH

TOP OF STOVE

1 head cauliflower, cooked whole
12 pieces broccoli, cooked
$^1/_4$ cup melted butter
Paprika

Place cooked cauliflower in center of round serving plate. Surround with broccoli. Pour melted butter over top. Sprinkle lightly with paprika. Makes 6 servings.

CORN CUSTARD

OVEN

2 eggs, well beaten
$^1/_2$ cup cracker crumbs
$^1/_4$ cup sugar
$^1/_2$ teaspoon salt
1 cup milk
1 (16-ounce) can cream style corn

Combine ingredients. Pour into buttered 1-quart baking dish. Bake at 350° for 35 to 40 minutes or until center is set. Makes 4 to 6 servings.

SNOW PEAS

TOP OF STOVE

2 packages frozen snow peas (or use fresh)
1 (8-ounce) can water chestnuts, drained and sliced
2 tablespoons butter
Dash garlic salt

Melt butter in skillet or wok. Add remaining ingredients. Cook until tender, but still crisp. Makes 4 servings.
TIP: If desired, add a few sliced mushrooms or onion rings.

MINTED PETITE PEAS

1 (10-ounce) package frozen baby peas in butter sauce
$^1/_4$ cup apple-mint jelly

Cooked peas according to directions. Stir in jelly until melted. Makes 4 servings.

HONEY GLAZED CARROTS

TOP OF STOVE
OVEN

> 6 large carrots, peeled
> Salt
> $^1/_4$ cup honey
> 1 cup (4-ounces) grated Cheddar cheese

Cut carrots in half crosswise. Cook in boiling salted water until just tender, about 15 minutes; drain. Roll each carrot in honey. Place in 1-quart greased baking dish; sprinkle with grated cheese. Bake at 350° for 5 to 10 minutes or until cheese is melted. Makes 4 servings.
TIP: For added color, sprinkle with finely chopped parsley.

COMPANY BAKED CARROTS

OVEN

My favorite carrot recipe

> 1 pound carrots, sliced diagonally into $^1/_2$-inch slices
> 3 tablespoons butter, sliced thin
> 1 tablespoon packed light brown sugar
> $^1/_2$ teaspoon salt
> $^1/_4$ teaspoon cracked pepper

Place carrots in $1^1/_2$-quart casserole. Distribute butter pieces over top. Sprinkle with brown sugar, salt and cracked pepper. Cover and bake at 350° for 1 hour or until carrots are tender. Makes 4 servings.

MUSTARD CARROTS

TOP OF STOVE

> 1 pound carrots
> $^1/_2$ cup butter or margarine
> $^1/_4$ cup firmly packed light brown sugar
> 1 teaspoon dry mustard
> Salt and pepper

Peel or scrape carrots; cut diagonally into $^1/_2$ inch slices. Melt butter in heavy saucepan. Add carrots along with remaining ingredients. Cook, stirring occasionally, until carrots are crisp tender and glazed. Makes 4 servings.
TIP: If desired, cut carrots in julienne strips.

CARROTS WITH BASIL   TOP OF STOVE

> 1 pound carrots, cut diagonally into $1/2$-inch slices
> 2 tablespoons butter or margarine, melted
> 2 tablespoons sliced almonds
> $1/4$ teaspoon salt
> $1/8$ teaspoon pepper
> $1/2$ teaspoon basil

Steam carrots until crisp tender. Combine remaining ingredients. Pour over carrots, tossing to coat. Makes 4 servings.
TIP: Asparagus, broccoli or brussel sprouts can be substituted for the carrots.

FRIED EGGPLANT   TOP OF STOVE

> 1 eggplant, cut in $1/2$ to 1-inch slices
> 2 tablespoons flour
> $1/2$ teaspoon baking powder
> 2 eggs, beaten
> 3 tablespoons water
> Oil or half oil and half butter

Combine flour, baking powder, eggs and water; mix thoroughly. Dip eggplant in batter; fry slowly in hot oil until nicely browned. Turn and brown other side. Cook a few slices at a time, adding more oil when necessary. Do not crowd pan.
TIP: If desired, sprinkle with salt, pepper and Parmesan cheese. An even easier method is to dust slices with flour, brown on both sides; season with salt and pepper.

POTATOES ANNA   OVEN

> 6 medium potatoes, peeled
> $1/2$ cup butter
> Salt and pepper

Slice potatoes into $1/8$-inch rounds. Generously butter a deep 10-inch pie dish. Arrange potatoes in the bottom, overlapping the slices spiral-fashion. Build up layers, dotting each layer with butter and seasoning with salt and pepper. Cover with foil and bake at 400° for 45 minutes. Remove foil and bake, uncovered, until potatoes are very tender and browned on top, usually about 20 to 30 minutes. The potatoes should be brown and crisp on the outside and tender and buttery on the inside. Invert on plate and serve. Makes 6 servings.

SWISS AU GRATIN POTATOES   OVEN

Rich and creamy. Serve with baked ham, green peas, Italian Salad, and sour dough rolls.

> 2 pounds (about 5 cups) potatoes, peeled, thinly sliced
> 1/4 cup butter, cut into small pieces
> 1 1/2 cups whipping cream
> Salt and pepper
> 1 cup (4-ounces) grated Swiss cheese

Place half of the potato slices in greased 2-quart shallow baking dish. Sprinkle with salt and pepper and half of the butter and cheese. Repeat layers ending with the cheese. Pour cream over top. Cover with foil. Bake at 325° for 1 hour 15 minutes. Remove foil and bake 30 to 45 minutes or until top is lightly browned and potatoes are tender.

AU GRATIN POTATOES   OVEN

> 1 can cream of chicken soup
> 2/3 cup milk
> 1 teaspoon salt
> 1/4 teaspoon pepper
> 6 potatoes, thinly sliced
> 1 cup (4-ounces) grated Cheddar cheese

Combine soup and milk, mixing until smooth. Add salt and pepper. Place half of potato slices in buttered 10x7-inch baking dish. Pour half of soup mixture over potatoes. Sprinkle with half of the grated cheese. Repeat layers. Cover with foil; bake at 350° for 1 hour. Uncover; bake 30 minutes or until golden and potatoes are tender. Makes 6 servings. TIP: If desired, add 1 small onion, finely chopped. For a main dish add 1 cup chicken, cut up.

GRILLED POTATOES   GRILL

> 3 large potatoes, peeled
> Salt and pepper
> 1 onion, sliced
> 2 cups (8-ounces) grated Cheddar cheese
> 1/2 cup butter, sliced

Slice potatoes in 1/4-inch slices. Divide potatoes and place in center of 4 large pieces of heavy duty foil. Sprinkle with salt and pepper. Top with onion slices, cheese and butter slices. Make butcher fold with foil; tightly seal ends. Place on grill and cook 45 to 60 minutes, turning packages several times. Serve in foil. Makes 4 servings.

EASY POTATO BAKE   OVEN

4 medium large potatoes
$1/2$ cup melted butter
Salt and pepper
Grated Parmesan cheese

Peel potatoes; slice $1/8$-inch thick. Place potatoes in shallow $1^1/2$-quart baking dish. Pour butter over top. Sprinkle with salt, pepper and Parmesan. Bake at 375° for 30 to 40 minutes or until tender. Makes 4 servings.

POTATO FANS   OVEN

4 medium potatoes, peeled
Salt and pepper
Melted butter

Stand potatoes on end and cut lengthwise slices $1/4$-inch thick, cutting slices to within 1 inch of bottom. Lay on side and spread potato as for a fan. Place on flat baking sheet; sprinkle with salt and pepper. Brush generously with melted butter. Bake at 400° for 45 minutes or until potatoes are tender, basting occasionally with butter. Makes 4 servings.

CRISS-CROSS POTATOES   OVEN

2 large baking potatoes, halved lengthwise
$1/4$ cup melted butter
Salt and pepper
Paprika

Score potatoes in crisscross pattern, making cut about 1 inch deep without cutting through skins. Brush with butter. Sprinkle with salt, pepper, and paprika. Place on baking sheet. Bake at 450° for 35 minutes or until done, basting occasionally with butter. Makes 4 servings.

EASY DINNER FRIES   TOP OF STOVE

Whole red potatoes (as many as desired)
Oil
Salt

Boil potatoes until tender - do not overcook. Cut into bite-size chunks, leaving peel on. Heat oil in heavy saucepan to 375°. Add potatoes (not too many at a time); cook until golden brown. Drain on paper towels. Sprinkle with salt.

OVEN FRENCH FRIES

2 large baking potatoes
1 tablespoon oil
$^1/_4$ teaspoon paprika
Salt

Scrub potatoes but do not peel. Cut in half lengthwise; cut each half into 6 to 8 wedges. Soak potatoes in cold water for 20 minutes; drain. Blot dry with paper towels. Place in small bowl; sprinkle oil and paprika over top. Toss to coat evenly. Arrange potatoes in single layer in greased shallow baking pan. Bake at 475° for about 20 minutes, stirring or turning to brown evenly. Cook until tender and lightly browned. Makes 4 servings.

PARTY BAKED POTATOES

Large baking potatoes
Your choice of:
    Butter
    Sour Cream
    Chopped green onions or chives
    Cooked and crumbled bacon
    Minced hard-cooked egg
    Grated Cheddar cheese

Cover each potato with foil and bake at 400° for 1 hour or until soft when squeezed. Slit top of potato through foil and press open. Serve potatoes and let each guest prepare their own from your choice of the above ingredients.

CHEESY POTATO STRIPS

3 large potatoes, cut as for French fries
$^1/_2$ cup milk
2 tablespoons butter
Salt and pepper
$^3/_4$ cup (3-ounces) grated Cheddar cheese
Chopped parsley

Place potato strips in greased 10x7-inch baking dish; pour milk over top. Dot with butter. Sprinkle with salt and pepper. Cover and bake at 425° for 45 minutes or until tender. Remove from oven; sprinkle with cheese and parsley. Return to oven and bake, uncovered, 10 minutes or until cheese is melted and most of the milk has been absorbed. Makes 4 servings.

NEW POTATOES WITH BUTTER SAUCE   TOP OF STOVE

> 2 pounds small new potatoes, peeled
> $1/4$ cup butter or margarine
> $1^1/_2$ teaspoons lemon juice
> Salt and pepper
> 1 teaspoon dried parsley

Cook whole potatoes in boiling salted water until tender, about 25 to 30 minutes. Meanwhile, melt butter with remaining ingredients. Drain potatoes; put in serving bowl. Pour butter mixture over top. Makes 4 servings.

STUFFED BAKED POTATOES   OVEN

> 4 large potatoes, baked
> Butter
> Salt and pepper
> $1/2$ cup sour cream
> $1/3$ cup cooked crumbled bacon
> $1/4$ cup finely chopped green onion

Cut baked potatoes in half lengthwise. Carefully remove potato pulp, leaving $1/4$-inch thick shell. Whip potatoes with butter; season with salt and pepper. Fold in sour cream and bacon. Fill potato shells; sprinkle top with green onion. If necessary, return to oven to reheat. Makes 8 servings.

CHEESE MIX FOR VEGETABLES

> 12 slices bacon, cooked and crumbled
> 1 cup sour cream
> $1/2$ cup butter or margarine, softened
> 2 tablespoons chopped green onion (green part)
> 2 cups (8-ounces) grated Cheddar cheese

Combine sour cream and butter; mix well. Stir in onion, grated cheese and about three-fourths of the crumbled bacon. Cover and store in refrigerator until ready to use.
VEGETABLES: Asparagus, broccoli, green beans, etc. Cook vegetables and put in baking dish. Top with some of the cheese mixture, sprinkle with reserved bacon. Bake at 350° until cheese melts.
BAKED POTATOES: Cut criss-cross cuts in hot baked potatoes. Top with some of the cheese mixture, sprinkle with some of the reserved bacon. Place on baking sheet and bake at 350° until cheese starts to melt.

CANDIED SWEET POTATOES OVEN

    Canned sweet potatoes, drained
    Butter
    Brown sugar
    Large marshmallows

Place desired number of sweet potatoes in shallow baking dish. Top generously with slices of butter. Sprinkle generously with brown sugar. Bake at 350° for 1 hour. Remove from oven. Top with marshmallows spaced 2 inches apart. Return to oven; bake until marshmallows are puffy and lightly browned (watch carefully).

OLD FASHIONED SWEET POTATOES TOP OF STOVE

    3 pound sweet potatoes, peeled
    $1/4$ cup butter
    $1/3$ cup sugar
    $3/4$ cup firmly packed light brown sugar
    1 teaspoon salt
    $1/2$ cup water

Cut potatoes in quarters or thick slices. Melt butter in large heavy frying pan or electric skillet. Add potatoes; sprinkle with sugar, brown sugar and salt. Add water. Cover and cook over medium heat for 20 minutes. Turn potatoes, cover and lower heat. Continue cooking 20 minutes, turning once or twice, until tender and richly glazed. Makes 6 servings.

FRIED RICE TOP OF STOVE

    1 cup uncooked long grain rice, cooked and chilled
    5 slices bacon, cut into $1/2$-inch pieces
    1 small onion, chopped
    $1/4$ cup soy sauce
    1 egg, beaten
    2 green onions, sliced

Heat large skillet or wok; add bacon and cook until partially browned. Add the onion and cook, stirring occasionally, until tender but not browned. Stir in soy sauce and rice. Push the rice to the sides; pour the egg into the middle. Cook until egg is done, stirring to scramble. Stir egg into the rice along with the green onions. Cook until heated through. Makes 6 servings.
TIP: This is a great dish for using leftovers such as diced pork, ham or sausage. For variety, add 1 cup bean sprouts and/or 1 can sliced water chestnuts, drained.

ONION-RICE CASSEROLE

TOP OF STOVE
OVEN

A unique way to combine onion and rice.

4 large mild sweet onions
$^1/_4$ cup butter or margarine
2 cups cooked rice
1 cup (4-ounces) grated Swiss cheese
$^2/_3$ cup half and half
$^1/_3$ cup grated Parmesan cheese

Thinly slice onions. You should have about 6 cups. Separate into rings. Heat butter in large skillet. Add onions and cook until tender and transparent, but not brown. Combine with rice, cheese and half and half. Pour into buttered 2-quart shallow casserole. Sprinkle Parmesan over top. Bake at 325° for 60 minutes or until liquid is absorbed and cheese is golden brown. Makes 6 servings.

RICE PILAF

TOP OF STOVE

$^1/_4$ cup butter or margarine
1 small onion, finely chopped
1 cup uncooked long grain rice
2 cups chicken broth
1 teaspoon salt
$^1/_8$ teaspoon pepper

Melt butter in medium saucepan. Add onion; sauté until tender, but not browned. Add rice; cook, stirring occasionally, until rice is golden. Stir in broth; bring to a boil. Add salt and pepper. Cover pan and reduce heat. Cook over low heat 15 to 20 minutes or until broth is absorbed and rice is tender. Makes 6 servings.
TIP: For Pine Nut Pilaf, add $^1/_4$ cup toasted pine nuts, or $^1/_2$ cup cooked peas and 4 slices cooked bacon, crumbled, just before serving.

RICE-CHEESE BAKE

TOP OF STOVE
OVEN

1 cup uncooked long grain rice, cooked
1 cup (4-ounces) grated Cheddar cheese
$1^1/_2$ cups milk
2 eggs, beaten
1 teaspoon salt
$^1/_8$ teaspoon pepper

Combine ingredients in large mixing bowl; toss gently to mix. Pour into greased $1^1/2$-quart shallow baking dish. Bake at 350° for 30 minutes. Makes 6 to 8 servings.

ALMOND RICE CASSEROLE   OVEN

$^1/_4$ cup butter
2 cans beef consomme
1 small can sliced mushrooms, with liquid
1 cup uncooked long grain rice
$^1/_2$ cup slivered almonds
$^1/_2$ package onion soup mix

Heat oven to 350°. Place butter in 9x13-inch baking dish; put in oven to melt. Remove; stir in remaining ingredients; mix well. Cover with foil; bake 1 to 1 $^1/_2$ hours or until liquid is absorbed and rice is tender. Fluff to mix. Makes 6 to 8 servings.

VERMICELLI AND RICE   TOP OF STOVE

$^1/_2$ cup vermicelli, broken into 1 to 1$^1/_2$-inch pieces, cooked and drained
$^1/_2$ cup long grain rice, cooked
2 tablespoons butter, melted
$^1/_4$ cup golden raisins
Salt and pepper to taste

Combine cooked vermicelli and rice. Combine with remaining ingredients, tossing gently to mix. Makes 3 to 4 servings.

WALNUT RICE   TOP OF STOVE

2 cups chicken broth
1 cup uncooked long grain rice
1 teaspoon butter
$^1/_3$ cup finely chopped walnuts

In medium saucepan, combine chicken broth and rice. Bring to a boil; reduce heat. Cover and cook 15 to 20 minutes or until liquid is absorbed and rice is tender. Gently stir in butter and walnuts. Makes 4 to 6 servings.

BAKED ACORN SQUASH   OVEN

Acorn squash
Butter
Light brown sugar
Nutmeg

Cut squash in half; remove seeds. Place a generous dab of butter in each cavity. Sprinkle with brown sugar and nutmeg. Place in shallow baking dish; bake at 375° for 45 minutes or until tender.

BAKED TOMATO HALVES
OVEN

3 large tomatoes
1 cup soft bread crumbs
2 tablespoons butter or margarine
$^1/_4$ teaspoon dried basil, crushed
Sour cream

Cut tomatoes in half crosswise; place cut side up in shallow baking dish. Combine remaining ingredients; sprinkle evenly on tomatoes. Bake at 350° for 20 minutes or until tomatoes are heated through but still firm. Top with a dab of sour cream just before serving. Makes 6 servings.

ESCALLOPED VEGETABLES
TOP OF STOVE
OVEN

8 ounces each of fresh broccoli, cauliflower and carrots
4 tablespoons butter or margarine
4 tablespoons flour
2 cups milk
1 cup (4-ounces) grated Swiss cheese
$^1/_4$ teaspoon salt

Cut vegetables into bite-size pieces. Lightly steam until tender but still crisp. Melt butter in medium saucepan. Stir in flour; cook 2 minutes. Remove from heat. Stir in milk; cook, stirring constantly, until thickened. Stir in grated cheese until melted and smooth. Add salt. Combine vegetables and cheese sauce and pour into a greased $1^1/_2$-quart casserole. Bake at 350° for 20 minutes or until heated through. Makes 6 servings.
TIP: You can use just one, two or all three of the vegetables. To garnish; sprinkle with toasted slivered almonds.

SHERRIED VEGETABLE DISH
TOP OF STOVE

2 cups onion, cut in thin wedges
3 tablespoons butter or margarine
$^1/_2$ pound fresh mushrooms, sliced
1 small green pepper, diced
3 tablespoons sherry
$^3/_4$ teaspoon salt

Cook onion in butter until crisp tender. Add remaining ingredients; cook until green pepper is tender but still crisp. Makes 4 to 6 servings.
TIP: An excellent accompaniment to a steak and baked potato dinner.

YAM AND APPLE CASSEROLE   TOP OF STOVE
                                                OVEN

    6 yams, cooked and peeled (or use canned)
    6 tart apples, peeled
    $1/2$ cup butter or margarine
    2 cups water
    1 cup sugar
    3 tablespoons cornstarch

Cut yams and apples in $1/2$-inch slices. Cut rounds in half crosswise. Layer in buttered 3-quart deep casserole, starting with apples and ending with yams. Combine butter and water in medium saucepan. Bring to a boil. Mix sugar with cornstarch; add just enough cold water to make a paste. Add to boiling water mixture, stirring constantly. Bring to a boil; remove from heat. Pour over yams. Bake at 350° for 50 to 60 minutes or until apples are tender. Makes 12 servings.
TIP: This is a large recipe, but is delicious served with turkey or ham.

ZUCCHINI-TOMATO CASSEROLE   OVEN

    2 medium zucchini, sliced
    Salt and pepper
    1 medium onion, thinly sliced
    1 green pepper, thinly sliced
    2 tomatoes, sliced
    $1^1/2$ cups (6-ounces) grated Cheddar cheese

Place zucchini slices in buttered 2-quart deep casserole dish; sprinkle with salt and pepper. Separate onion slices into rings and spread on top of zucchini. Top with green pepper rings and tomato slices. Sprinkle grated cheese evenly over top. Bake, uncovered, at 350° for 60 minutes. Makes 6 servings.
TIP: This is an attractive dish to serve with almost anything. If you want the vegetables crispy tender, watch baking time carefully; if you prefer the vegetables soft and juicy, cook a few minutes longer.

ZUCCHINI AND TOMATOES   TOP OF STOVE

    2 small zucchini, sliced
    1 large onion, sliced
    2 tablespoons butter or margarine
    2 small tomatoes, cut into wedges
    $1/2$ teaspoon garlic salt
    $1/8$ teaspoon pepper

Cook zucchini and onion in heated butter until just crisp tender. Add remaining ingredients and cook 2 minutes. Makes 4 servings.
VARIATION: Omit pepper; sprinkle with grated Mozzarella cheese.

SAUTEÉD MUSHROOMS   TOP OF STOVE

8 ounces fresh mushrooms, slice or leave whole
1 medium onion, coarsely chopped
2 tablespoons butter or margarine
1 tablespoon oil

Heat butter and oil in skillet until hot (watch carefully so it doesn't burn). Add mushrooms and onions; sauté, stirring frequently, 4 to 5 minutes or until lightly browned. Makes 4 servings.

VEGETABLE STIR FRY   TOP OF STOVE

3 tablespoons butter or margarine
1 medium onion, cut into wedges, separated
1 cup sliced carrots
1¹/₂ cups fresh broccoli pieces
1¹/₂ cups sliced fresh mushrooms
3 tablespoons sherry

Heat butter in large skillet or wok. Add onion and carrots. Cook until crisp tender. Add remaining ingredients and cook, stirring occasionally, until broccoli is crisp tender. Serve immediately. Makes 4 servings.

ONIONS AND PEPPERS   TOP OF STOVE

Excellent served with Fajitas, hamburgers and steaks.

1¹/₂ tablespoons oil
¹/₄ teaspoon paprika
¹/₂ red pepper, cut into narrow strips
¹/₂ green pepper, cut into narrow strips
2 onions, thinly sliced, separated into rings
Salt and pepper to taste

Heat oil in large skillet. Stir in paprika. Add peppers and onion. Cook, stirring frequently, until vegetables are crisp tender

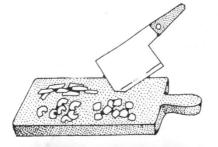

COOKBOOKS MAKE GREAT GIFTS

Have one or more on hand for:

Birthday	Showers	First Home
Christmas	Thank you gifts	Campers
Mother's Day	Weddings	Boaters

If books cannot be purchased locally , order forms may be used.

● ●

SIX INGREDIENTS OR LESS
P.O. BOX 922
GIG HARBOR, WA 98335

Please send me_____copies at ....$9.95 each $ _____
Plus Postage and handling.......................$1.25 each $ _____
Washington residents add sales tax.............70 each $ _____
Enclosed is my check or money order ....**Total** $ _____

PLEASE PRINT OR TYPE

NAME _____

ADDRESS _____

CITY _____STATE _____ZIP _____

● ●

SIX INGREDIENTS OR LESS
P.O. BOX 922
GIG HARBOR, WA 98335

Please send me_____copies at ....$9.95 each $ _____
Plus Postage and handling.......................$1.25 each $ _____
Washington residents add sales tax.............70 each $ _____
Enclosed is my check or money order ....**Total** $ _____

PLEASE PRINT OR TYPE

NAME _____

ADDRESS _____

CITY _____STATE _____ZIP _____